W9-CFO-862

A Heart Like Mary's

Mary, Give us Your heart!

Fr Edward Looney

"*A Heart Like Mary's* is a marvelous blend of scripture, reflection, personal experience, and inspiration. Fr. Looney's gift for helping others draw closer to Mary shines in this work, and his great love for her is absolutely contagious. No one can pray through this book without acquiring a deeper love and yearning for the Blessed Virgin Mother."

Marge Fenelon
Author of *Imitating Mary* and *Our Lady, Undoer of Knots*

"Mary is straightforward. Mary is profound. This book is the same. We are indebted to Fr. Looney, who has made the profound so accessible. The reader will come to know Mary and learn how to imitate her incredible virtues."

Msgr. Charles M. Mangan
Office of the Marian Apostolate
Diocese of Sioux Falls

"Anyone can benefit from Fr. Edward Looney's insightful meditations on Our Lady. I believe this book will help many people acquire a more tender and loving heart like Mary's."

Rev. Donald H. Calloway, M.I.C.
Author of *Champions of the Rosary*

"Popes and saints say that the heart most like the Sacred Heart is the heart of Mary. Through scriptural reflections, approved Marian apparitions, and daily action items, Fr. Looney has given us a prayerful, engaging, and practical way to make our hearts more like the hearts of Jesus and Mary."

Rev. James Kubicki, S.J.
Author of *A Heart On Fire* and *A Year of Daily Offerings*

"*A Heart Like Mary's* is a thirty-one-day yes to God. Fr. Edward Looney lives out a mature devotion to the Holy Mother. He shares a month of meditations, prayers, and challenges that will inspire you to the humility, obedience, and love found in the heart of Mary."

Stacy A. Trasancos
Author of *Particles of Faith*

"This book by Rev. Edward Looney is one of the best applied guides in Marian spirituality I have ever seen. It is concerned more with practice than theory, and it embodies the teaching of Jesus in the Sermon on the Mount: 'Blessed are the pure of heart, for they will see God.' Many graces will come to those who read this book prayerfully and faithfully. It provides a thirty-one-day journey toward purity of heart with Mary's heart as the inspiration and guide. Fr. Looney's book helps us realize the depth and wisdom of the message of Fatima where Mary said, 'In the end, my Immaculate Heart will triumph.'"

Robert L. Fastiggi
Professor of Systematic Theology at Sacred Heart Major Seminary
Former president of the Mariological Society of America

"Fr. Edward Looney is a priest who loves Mary. He knows how much sweeter life is when you know her motherly love. A *Heart Like Mary's* is a practical guide to living in her heart, which leads directly to the heart of her son. We'll be a more tender people when we let her show us the heart of her son. Embracing her love as her sons and daughters, too, goes a long way toward our transformation into people truly living in the freedom of Christ, living the Beatitudes. Thank you, Fr. Looney, for the help!"

Kathryn Jean Lopez
Senior fellow at the National Review Institute

A Heart Like Mary's

31 Daily Meditations to Help You Live and Love as She Does

EDWARD LOONEY

AVE MARIA PRESS AVE Notre Dame, Indiana

Nihil Obstat: Very Rev. John W. Girotti, J.C.L.

Imprimatur: +Most Reverend David L. Ricken, D.D., J.C.L.
                 Bishop of Green Bay

Unless marked otherwise, scripture quotations are from *New Revised Standard Version Bible*, copyright © 1989 National Council of the Churches of Christ in the United States of America. Used by permission. All rights reserved.

© 2017 by Edward Looney

All rights reserved. No part of this book may be used or reproduced in any manner whatsoever, except in the case of reprints in the context of reviews, without written permission from Ave Maria Press®, Inc., P.O. Box 428, Notre Dame, IN 46556, 1-800-282-1865.

Founded in 1865, Ave Maria Press is a ministry of the United States Province of Holy Cross.

www.avemariapress.com

Paperback: ISBN-13 978-1-59471-783-3

E-book: ISBN-13 978-1-59471-784-0

Cover image © iStockphoto.com.

Cover and text design by Christopher D. Tobin.

Printed and bound in the United States of America.

Library of Congress Cataloging-in-Publication Data is available.

To all those in my life
from whom I have learned what it
means to live with a Marian heart.

Prayer of St. Teresa of Calcutta

Mary, my dearest Mother, give me your heart, so beautiful, so pure, so immaculate, so full of love and humility. That I may receive Jesus as you did and go in haste to give him to others.

Contents

Introduction: A Marian Heart

The Church recently observed the hundredth anniversary of the Fatima apparitions. In 1916 the Angel of Portugal appeared to the three shepherd children and Our Lady appeared six times between May and October 1917. To celebrate their centennial anniversary, the sanctuary produced an official symbol for the year: a gigantic heart sculpture containing a mirror near the bottom of the heart. As you stand close to the heart and look up to the mirror you find yourself in the heart of Mary. I had the opportunity to visit Fatima in September 2016, just as the anniversary celebrations were beginning. As I stood below the heart sculpture, a sense of gratitude welled up within me: gratitude that I, a son of Mary, was a part of Mary's heart. After all, this is the heart that treasured the moments of Jesus' life. Now as our mother, she treasures the happenings of our lives in her heart. This image is true—we can find ourselves in the heart of Mary. The inverse also is true: we want to find Mary's heart in ours. Her heart is a two-way mirror.

This is the premise of the book you now hold, born out of an unforgettable experience with my spiritual director while in the seminary. He was a Mariologist, and I was a student of Mariology, a lover of the Madonna. Believe it or not, I have a tendency at times to be overly critical, negative, and pessimistic (I'm working on that!), and he called me out one day. He said, "You love Mary so much, but where is your Marian heart?" After that exchange, in my prayer each morning I began to ask God to give me a heart like his mother's. Over time, I reflected on what it means to have a Marian heart. I came up with a few attributes, which I asked for each day in prayer. At the end of my morning holy hour, I would pray something similar to this: "Mary, give me a heart like yours, attentive to the needs of others, generous, loving, and pure. Help me to treasure what happens today in the depths of my heart and to make intercession for others."

This book, which really is a journey into Mary's heart, was shaped by experiences from my personal prayer after I received the inspiration from Our Lady to write it. In March 2015, I published *A Rosary Litany*, and afterward I told Our Lady I was going to retire for some time before writing again. But I felt Mary tugging on my heart. One day, as I prayed before the Blessed Sacrament, I prayed the prayer asking for a Marian heart, and I was struck with the outline for *A Heart Like Mary's*. I knew in the depths of my heart Mary was asking me to share my experience of her heart so that others too might possess a heart like hers. Like Our Lady, I offered my fiat, my yes, and this book came to birth.

A Heart Like Mary's is intended for any person who wants to experience a greater transformation of heart. The persistent call of Jesus in the scriptures and that of Our Lady in her many apparitions is one of conversion. As related earlier, this book emerged out of my dissatisfaction with the state of my own heart, which for a time was embittered, pessimistic, and negative. I desired what the prophet Ezekiel (36:26) wrote about: I wanted God to take away my stony heart and give me a natural heart. As a Catholic, I turned to Mary, who was mother and teacher to the Son of God, to teach me how to have a new heart. I entered into the heart of Mary and, little by little, the bitterness and pessimism grew less, and I became more positive.

As I reflected on the heart of Mary I found many attributes I wanted to attain. I also began to realize that the goal of humanity should be to possess a heart like hers, because hers is the exemplar for all human hearts. Our hearts are prone to concupiscence on account of original sin, but her heart is sinless, immaculate, and pure. Mary's heart is capable of pure love of God and for others. This is precisely what I wanted. I desired to love Jesus as she loved Jesus and to love my neighbor as she loved her neighbor. This is what the heart of our Mother wants for you and me—to love. We want to have a heart like hers, to have her attributes and desires. If you are like me, there are areas in the spiritual life you can improve during this thirty-one-day journey. Whenever we exercise, we strain our heart for a short time, but the work proves beneficial for our long-term health. Similarly, as we strive to attain a heart like Mary's, our hearts will be exercised, causing an increase in charity. A healthy spiritual heart will form that will remain a part of us.

The format of *A Heart Like Mary's* is straightforward—thirty-one meditations meant for daily use. Throughout the calendar year, the Church observes two months as principally Marian—May and October—which, coincidentally, both have thirty-one days and which mark the beginning and end of the Marian apparitions in Fatima. During the month of May, I typically try to take on an extra Marian devotion as a way to honor Mary. Perhaps a journey into Mary's heart would be appropriate. A reader could also use this book, starting thirty-one days ahead of time, to prepare for a major Marian feast day. If begun on May 1, the book would conclude on the feast of the Visitation. Or maybe it would be fitting to use this book as a way to prepare for the Feast of the Immaculate Heart of Mary, a moveable feast, whose date is the third Saturday following Pentecost. Each individual reader can decide for him- or herself when they wish to begin the journey into the heart of Mary.

This thirty-one-day journey will be twofold: to discover, first, the attributes of Mary's heart, as derived from the scriptures, and second, the desires of Mary's heart, made known through approved private revelations. The first part will span twenty-one days, or three weeks; the last ten days will be dedicated to the second part. Each day will provide a scriptural quote or a message from Our Lady's apparitions, followed by a reflection leading you into the depths of Mary's heart and showing you how her heart can be mirrored in yours. After the reflection, you will be invited to call upon Mary's intercession, asking her to give you a heart like hers. The daily meditation concludes with a challenge to live with a Marian heart. It simply is not enough to reflect on the heart of Mary. Reflection must lead to action and the cultivation of a heart like hers.

If you are ready for a life-changing experience, I invite you to journey into the heart of Mary. There you will discover her heart's attributes and desires, and with the help of Mary, through her intercession and example, you will begin to have a heart like hers.

Part I

Attributes of Mary's Heart

Part one of our Marian journey focuses on attributes of Mary's heart. The twenty-one attributes identified are not exhaustive. I'm almost certain that people could recommend many more characteristics of Mary's heart. Each of the reflections takes its inspiration from an aspect of Mary's life with Jesus as derived from the sacred scriptures. During this twenty-one-day journey, as we examine a different characteristic each day, the goal is to incorporate the day's attribute into your daily life. The aim of course is not isolated to one day only but to last for the rest of our lives—to live every day with a heart like Mary's. As you prepare to begin this journey, prayerfully ask Mary to pray for you as you strive to live and love as she did while on earth and still does from her throne in heaven.

Day One

A Heart Patiently Waiting

Scripture

> *In the sixth month the angel Gabriel was sent by God to a town in Galilee called Nazareth, to a virgin engaged to a man whose name was Joseph, of the house of David. The virgin's name was Mary.*
>
> —Luke 1:26–27

Reflection

If you search Google or your preferred Internet search engine for images of the annunciation, you will find likenesses captured by the great painters of history. Oftentimes these paintings contain projections of the artist from their historical time period, depicting Mary kneeling at a *prie-dieu* and reading from a codex book or praying the Rosary. Each of these paintings depicts Mary as a faithful daughter of Israel. She is the Daughter of Zion whom the prophets Zechariah (2:10, 9:9) and Zephaniah (3:14) foretold. As a Jewish woman, Mary waited with all of Israel for the coming of the promised one, the Messiah, who would save them from their sins. She knew the Messiah would come, and so with her ancestors she waited.

Many of these artists depict Mary reading from a book, presumably the Old Testament. In that moment, as she patiently waited and read those sacred words, what did she read? Maybe she read the prophecy of Isaiah 7:14, of how a virgin would give birth to a son and call him Emmanuel. Or maybe she reflected on the story of creation, of Adam and Eve, and how a woman would crush the head of a serpent (Gn 3:15). Perhaps she read about the enclosed garden in the Song of Songs (4:12) or Ezekiel's closed gate (44:2). If she read any of those passages, maybe she understood that soon they would be fulfilled. Israel's waiting would be over. For Mary is that Virgin; she is the new Eve; she is the enclosed garden; she is the closed gate.

The patient daughter of Israel is interrupted in her reading, in her reflection, by the angel who announces Israel must wait no longer. This patient daughter forces us who now read and reflect on the annunciation to wait, as St. Bernard of Clairvaux reflected, "The angel awaits your reply, for it is time that he should return to God, Who sent him. We, too, are waiting" (*Missus Est,* IV.14). When we gaze at those depictions, we patiently wait with the angel Gabriel for her answer, because salvation is at hand. Mary, the one who reflected on God's word, receives the one who is *the* Word into her very being.

We live in a very fast-paced culture of drive-thrus and multitasking. When someone or something slows us down, we become impatient. Mary can teach us what it means to be patient. Mary also fits the other understanding of being patient: to tolerate. Mary is patient with us even today as she comes to earth with a message calling sinful humanity back to her son. We are slow to learn and understand, but with Jesus, she patiently waits for the conversion of our hearts. Sit with the example of Mary's patience, and ask how you can become more like her. Be patient while you wait for the revelation of God's plan for your life or for an answer to your prayers. Be patient with those around you. Allow Mary to teach you patience.

Prayer to Mary Our Intercessor

Mary, my mother, give me a heart like yours; help me to patiently wait through life, especially as I wait for the day your son calls me home to be with him.

Today's Step toward Living with a Marian Heart

Today when you find yourself impatient while waiting in line, stuck in traffic, or listening to another person, remember Mary and ask God for the gift of patience.

Day Two

A Heart Seeking Clarity

Mary Speaks

How shall this be, since I have no husband?
—Luke 1:34 (RSV)

Reflection

It's not always easy for me to understand or accept what God is doing with my life. I sometimes find myself questioning him, thinking, "Really God? You want me to do what?" This was the case with my journey in the seminary. I went to seminary right out of high school. For two years that had been all I wanted for my life, and so I expected it to be the best experience of my life. But it wasn't. After just a few weeks there, I asked myself, "Did I make the right decision? Why did I come here?" At the semester's end, I applied to a college back home and left the seminary. I believed, "I gave God his chance, and now I can do whatever I want with my life." A little over a year later, God came knocking again. Even though I loved my new field of study, I found that it was not fulfilling me. As I thought back, I realized the only thing that fulfilled me was doing churchy things! I started talking with vocation directors, and, well, I ended up back in the seminary. I was going to a different seminary, further away from my home, at a Benedictine monastery. In the days before I was to leave for the seminary, I began to doubt and question my life change: "God, do you really want me to go back to seminary? Don't you remember what it was like the first time? It's not for me. Why am I going to this seminary?" God answered all the questions I asked in the weeks, months, and years that I spent in seminary. I needed God to clarify what he was asking of me, and he did it in his time and in his way. Maybe you've found yourself in this same position of uncertainty. Such questions are not expressions of doubt in God's love, necessarily, but rather moments that require faith and trust in God's will.

When our hearts seek clarity, it means we have been listening for the voice of God in the recesses of our heart. If we were not listening to God, we would not have these questions. Mary listened intently to what the angel Gabriel said to her. After hearing she was to be the mother of God, she did not understand how it could be, for she had had no relations with a man. She probably thought to herself, "Really, God? You want me to do what?" Yet she asks the question and receives a response: "The Holy Spirit will come upon you, and the power of the Most High will overshadow you" (Lk 1:35). Another instance of Mary seeking clarity was at the finding of Jesus in the temple. She asks Jesus, "Son, why have you treated us so? Behold, your father and I have been looking for you anxiously" (Lk 2:48). She does not understand the situation, and so she seeks clarity from her Son.

In 1859, the Queen of Heaven appeared to Adele Brise in a small Belgian settlement near the Door Peninsula in Wisconsin. Adele sought clarity in two different ways: seeking counsel first from her parish priest and then from the Mother of God herself. Adele saw the Blessed Mother twice before she conversed with her heavenly visitor. After the second vision, which happened on the way to Mass, Adele knew she needed help, so she sought direction from her pastor. After sharing what transpired, he instructed her to ask the lady, "In God's name, who are you and what do you want of me?" That's precisely what Adele did. During the third apparition, Mary commended her for attending Mass and requested she make a general confession and offer her communion for the conversion of sinners. Then Mary asked Adele poignant questions, for which Adele sought clarity. Mary asked Adele, "Why are you standing here in idleness while your companions are working in the vineyard of the Lord?" Adele sought clarification: "What more can I do, dear lady?" She listened but needed more information, and that is when Mary relayed the mission of catechesis to her: "Gather the children in this wild country and teach them what they should know for salvation."

If there is some quandary in your life, know that you are not alone. Adele provides us with an example of what it means to seek clarity. Sometimes when God asks us to do something (or, in her case, the Blessed Mother does the asking) we might require guidance from a trusted person. Sometimes we might feel unqualified or believe the task to be impossible, and with Mary we might ask, "How can this be?" There is an answer to our question: God's wonderful and marvelous plan for us.

Prayer to Mary Our Intercessor

Mary, my mother, give me a heart like yours, a heart seeking clarity, a heart listening to God's voice, so I can see God's marvelous plan for my life.

Today's Step toward Living with a Marian Heart

Do you have a major decision to make? Is something weighing heavily on you? A friendship, a request to do something? Spend a few moments in prayer listening for the voice of God. Do not be afraid to ask God where he is leading you or what you are supposed to do.

Day Three

A Chaste Heart

Scripture

A garden locked is my sister, my bride, a garden locked, a fountain sealed.

—Song of Solomon 4:12

Reflection

The Church teaches dogmatically that Mary was a perpetual virgin, meaning she remained a virgin before, during, and after the birth of Jesus. Many theologians argue Mary took a vow of virginity before the annunciation, signifying that her heart was virginal, pure, and chaste.

Mary's chastity can inspire our modern-day culture, which perverts sexuality. Turn on any television show or movie today and you will surely find the glorification of immorality. Many characters engage in pre-marital sex, adultery, and polygamous relationships. There is your token homosexual, bisexual, or now transgender character. Such things have become so commonplace that we no longer question it when we see it in the shows or movies we watch.

The proliferation of pornography continues to plague many men and women. Scientists now understand the harmful effects pornography has on a person: it rewires the brain. In addition to being genuinely addictive, pornography leads to objectifying women, to devaluing the dignity of the human person, and to viewing the other person as an object for gratification.

The Shrine of Our Lady of Guadalupe in La Crosse, Wisconsin, houses a beautiful mural of St. Maria Goretti. Many people know the story of St. Maria Goretti, who died as a martyr of chastity and purity. Alessandro, an eighteen-year-old with many issues, who lived nearby the Goretti household, became obsessed with Maria to the point that one day he attempted to rape Maria. Maria resisted the attack not only to defend her own chastity but also because she was concerned for the salvation of her attacker. She kept yelling to Alessandro, "It is a sin. God forbids it. You will go to hell, Alessandro. You will go to hell if you do it." Even though she was being attacked, her concern was for the eternal well-being of Alessandro.

Maria's resistance infuriated Alessandro, and he stabbed Maria fourteen times. The wounds were too much for Maria; she died the following day, after forgiving

Alessandro for his crime. Alessandro had difficulty in forgiving himself for Maria's death. One night, while he was in prison, Maria appeared to him in a dream and gave him fourteen lilies as a gesture of forgiveness, symbolic of the fourteen wounds she had suffered at Alessandro's hand. At the Shrine of Our Lady of Guadalupe, the mural depicts St. Maria Goretti presenting the lilies to Alessandro, with Mary in the background. While Mary did not appear with St. Maria Goretti in Alessandro's dream, Mary appears in the background for a few reasons: first, because Maria's family was devoted to the Blessed Virgin, and second, because Mary is the example of purity *par excellence.*

The same vice to which Alessandro succumbed, resulting in Maria's death, actively claims souls today. Many souls fall victim to pornography, fornication, and adulterous relationships. But Mary, the pure one, wants to crush this evil in the world. The antidote to the attack on purity is a chaste Marian heart. Having a chaste heart means we see people not as objects but rather as sons and daughters of God, brothers and sisters in Jesus. We try to love each and every person for whom he or she is. To have a chaste heart is to want others also to have a chaste heart. As a result, we dress modestly so as not to lead them into sin. It also means keeping custody of our eyes, the windows to our soul. Last, a chaste heart speaks purely and strives not to tell impure or crude jokes.

Many people in our society today struggle with issues related to chastity. As we try to live with a Marian heart every day, it is important for us to recommit ourselves to living with a chaste and pure heart. If it has been a while since you went to the sacrament of Penance, go and confess the sins of your past, and receive forgiveness. Then commit yourself every day to living with a chaste heart, and if there are times when you slip up, run back to the Lord and ask for forgiveness. Also, it is important to forgive ourselves for the sins of our past. That's what Alessandro struggled with when St. Maria Goretti appeared to him. Ask God to purify your mind and your heart from any impurity of the past, so that your memories do not become an obstacle to living with a chaste heart. We cannot change our past; we can only live in the present moment committed to live minute by minute, day by day, with a chaste heart.

Our culture needs the prayers of Mary so that all people will strive to live chastely and purely. Her prayers will be answered if we begin to change our lives and live with chaste hearts. It begins with you and with me—with one person at a time.

Prayer to Mary Our Intercessor

Mary, my mother, give me a heart like yours, a chaste heart, capable of loving everyone I meet.

Today's Step toward Living with a Marian Heart

Conduct a short examination of conscience regarding the type of clothing you wear, the words you speak, and the shows or movies you watch. Do they help you to have a chaste heart like Mary's? Is God calling you to conversion of life? How will you answer?

Day Four
A Heart That Says Yes

Scripture

> *Then Mary said, "Here am I, the servant of the Lord;*
> *let it be with me according to your word." Then the*
> *angel departed from her.*
>
> —Luke 1:38

Reflection

Mary heard everything God's messenger relayed to her. As she listened, the message prompted a response within her heart. She wanted there to be no ambiguity as to her role in this salvific act. The angel did not ask Mary, "Will you do this?" But from the depth of her heart, Mary proclaims what we call her fiat—Let it be with me—her *yes* to God!

In our life we are faced with many decisions. We really have only two responses that we can give to a myriad of situations: yes or no.

We can say *yes* to getting up when our first alarm goes off, or we can say *no*.

We can say *yes* and speak to the stranger we pass by, or we can simply continue on our way.

We can say *yes* to doing our daily tasks, or we can waste our time uselessly.

We can say *yes* to spending a few moments in prayer each day, or we can say *no* and turn on our favorite video-streaming provider.

We can say *yes* to going to Mass each Sunday, or we can say *no*, making time to do other things.

In the Christian life, it can be difficult to say yes. As we reflected earlier, sometimes we need to seek clarity because we feel unworthy of the task or think that it is impossible. That is when we need to say yes. It is very easy to say yes when something does not require much of us. It is difficult to say yes when something is hard. We might have to say yes to ending a relationship that deters us from living the gospel. Sometimes we have to say yes to suffering: "Yes, Lord, I will live with this disease and place my trust and hope in you."

Many times I have grappled with making a difficult decision and waffled back and forth. I am often unwilling to give up my spare time, especially on my day off. You might say I'm selfish with my time. Sometimes, though, there are certain things I ought to do even if the time is not convenient for me. In one of the cities where I have served, a young person committed suicide, and the funeral, at a local Lutheran Church, happened to be on my day off. I did not know the girl, but I thought I should go to the funeral, at the very least, to see which youth from the parish attended the funeral, so we could do follow-up pastoral care with them. It also happened that this funeral occurred during the Year of Mercy, so it was a good way to live out the corporal and spiritual works of mercy by going to the funeral and praying for the young person's soul and for those left behind. Afterward, when I was walking to my car, I said to myself, "This is exactly where I needed to be." It was the realization that I had said yes to God and done what I was supposed to do.

Mary's heart can teach us to say yes. If we learn from her heart what it means to say yes, moments of deliberation and doubt will be fewer. Then when we are able to say yes in small things, we will then say yes to larger things. When we say yes to prayer and service, we are really saying yes to God. And when we say yes to God, you can be certain he will keep asking. When he does, hopefully we can say yes!

Prayer to Mary Our Intercessor

Mary, my mother, give me a heart like yours, a heart that says yes to whatever God asks and to whomever God sends me. Expand my heart with your love so I will always say fiat!

Today's Step toward Living with a Marian Heart

When someone asks for your help today, or your conscience encourages you to complete your day's work, say yes without hesitation. Don't overthink it or try to weasel out of it. Just say yes!

Day Five

A Heart Filled with Generous Love

Scripture

> *In those days Mary set out and went with haste to a Judean town in the hill country, where she entered the house of Zechariah and greeted Elizabeth.*
>
> —Luke 1:39–40

Reflection

When the angel Gabriel appeared to Mary, he greeted her as *full of grace* and told her she had found favor with God. God granted Mary the singular privilege of being immaculately conceived, that is to say, without original sin. God foresaw the merits of the salvific work of Jesus and applied it to Mary from the moment of her conception in the womb of St. Anne. In this way, Mary already experienced the generous love of our God that we call mercy.

Mary listened to the words of the angel and heard the miraculous happenings in the life of Elizabeth, that this aged woman was now with child. The account of the annunciation closes, and Luke immediately follows it with Mary's setting out and going with haste to visit Elizabeth. Her reasons for going do not include a selfish need to have her faith reassured; she goes because her heart is filled with generous love. In fact, she does not casually go but rather sets out in haste, hurriedly, knowing that someone needs help. Further, she does not go for just a few days but remains for three months, offering assistance to Elizabeth. Mary's heart overflows with love as she pours herself out in service to someone in need. She forgets herself and focuses on the other.

By her Immaculate Conception, Mary shows herself to be a recipient of God's mercy. At the Visitation, Mary becomes an agent of God's mercy. The same is true for each one of us. Each time we receive Jesus in the Eucharist or Jesus' forgiveness in the confessional, we become recipients of God's generous love, his mercy. God truly has been generous toward us. He sent Jesus to be our savior. Before Jesus died, he shared another sign of his love by instituting the Eucharist. His generous love for all was in the blood he shed on the Cross, winning for us our salvation. God has done so much good for us that, in return, we must show that love to others. We must become like Mary, filled with God's love and bringing it to others.

Today we are called to have a heart filled with generous love. St. John of the Cross famously said, "In the evening of life we will be judged on love alone" (*Dichos*, 64, in *CCC*, 1022). Be generous in your love, like the Blessed Mother was, and surely at the end of our life, our good deeds will follow us into eternal life, where we will give an account of how we loved.

Prayer to Mary Our Intercessor

Mary, my mother, give me a heart like yours, a generous heart. Just as I have received God's love, help me to show that love to everyone I meet.

Today's Step toward Living with a Marian Heart

In the next week, find an opportunity to serve someone in need, just as Mary did for Elizabeth. Do you have an elderly neighbor or relative who could use help? Give them a call and find out if they could use some assistance. If they say no, consider dropping in with some flowers and fresh bread to brighten their day.

Day Six

A Heart That Praises God

Scripture

And Mary said, "My soul magnifies the Lord, and my spirit rejoices in God my Savior."

—Luke 1:46–47

Reflection

When Mary hears the words of her cousin Elizabeth, "Blessed are you among women, and blessed is the fruit of your womb. . . . And blessed is she who believed that there would be a fulfilment of what was spoken to her by the Lord," she immediately turns the praise back to God (Lk 1:42, 45). Hers is a heart that knows to whom the glory belongs. In turning the praise back to God, Mary reveals the humility of her heart.

Priests, deacons, consecrated religious, and laity alike remember Mary's song of praise each evening as they recite their Evening Prayer from the Liturgy of the Hours. Mary's song of praise is called the *Magnificat*, meaning "to magnify or glorify." There are remarkable similarities between

Mary's Magnificat and the song of Hannah in 1 Samuel
2:1–10. Some scholars suggest the similarities between
Mary's and Hannah's songs of praise provide evidence that
Mary knew the Hebrew scriptures, and readily recites her
hymn of praise.

In her Magnificat, Mary tells how God worked
throughout the history of Israel, by scattering the proud
and putting down the mighty from their thrones; by filling
the hungry with good things and sending the rich away
empty.

When something good happens in your life, a job
promotion or a unique opportunity, do you place all the
honor on yourself? Or do you acknowledge that God is the
giver of all that is good, and thus thank God for the favors
bestowed on you?

The Magnificat contains praise for the name of God
when Mary prays, "and holy is his name." Go to any sport-
ing event, and I guarantee you will hear the name of God
taken in vain. Do we revere the holiness of God's name?
A heart that praises God reveres the name of God. Be on
guard for moments when you do not praise God's holy
name. Always strive to invoke God's name as a prayer.

Mary also praises God for coming to the help of
Israel. In our own lives, God comes to our help each day.
We receive many graces from God. Sometimes God might

send us just the right person in our moment of need. Offer praise to God for the help he has shown you.

Occasionally we might find it difficult to praise God in the immediacy of the moment. Maybe something does not go the way we want it to, and we become angry with God. When I left seminary after just one semester and went home to a local college, I was studying political science. I thought it might be advantageous for me to start getting involved in politics, so I put my name in for a local non-partisan race. On election night, my opponent defeated me. I was humbled by the support I received and by the people who put their confidence in me, but I was upset that I lost. You could say it was difficult for me to praise God at that particular moment. Had I won election though, would I have been open to how God would work in my life? Would I have gone back to seminary? It is moments like these that leave us looking back, years later, and praising God for guiding the course of our life events.

Prayer to Mary Our Intercessor

Mary, my mother, give me a heart like yours, a heart that praises God. Help me to praise God for his presence throughout the day, for the past, and for what God will do in my life in years to come.

Today's Step toward Living with a Marian Heart

Slowly and prayerfully read Mary's Magnificat, and then ask yourself: How has God worked in my life? For what do I want to praise God? Take some time today and write (or pray) your own version of the Magnificat, specific to your life and circumstances.

> My soul magnifies the Lord,
>   and my spirit rejoices in God my Savior,
> for he has looked with favor on the lowliness
>   of his servant.
> Surely, from now on all generations will call
>   me blessed;
> for the Mighty One has done great things for
>   me,
>   and holy is his name.
> His mercy is for those who fear him
>   from generation to generation.
> He has shown strength with his arm;
>   he has scattered the proud in the thoughts
>   of their hearts.
> He has brought down the powerful from their
>   thrones,
> and lifted up the lowly;
> he has filled the hungry with good things,
>   and sent the rich away empty.
> He has helped his servant Israel,

in remembrance of his mercy,
according to the promise he made to our
    ancestors,
to Abraham and to his descendants forever.
                                    —Luke 1:46–55

Day Seven

A Humble Heart

Mary Speaks

*He has brought down the powerful from their
thrones, and lifted up the lowly.*

—Luke 1:52

Reflection

The original sin committed by Adam and Eve was caused
by pride. They heard God's instruction but believed they
knew better. Instead of being humble before the law of
God, they tried to be above it. In our tradition, we call
Jesus and Mary the New Adam and the New Eve, for they
undo the damage from our first parents' downfall. In this,
both Jesus and Mary provide an example of humility con-
quering pride.

Mary became the humble servant of the Lord when
she rendered her fiat during the annunciation. She said,
"Here am I, the servant of the Lord." In calling herself a
servant, she spoke about her lowliness. This is precisely

what she proclaims in the Magnificat, that God cast down the powerful from their thrones and exalted the lowly.

In his letter to the Philippians, St. Paul points out the humility of Christ: "Though he was in the form of God, [he] did not regard equality with God as something to be exploited, but emptied himself, taking the form of a slave, being born in human likeness. And being found in human form, he humbled himself and became obedient to the point of death—even death on a cross" (Phil 2:6–8). Jesus Christ, God incarnate, humbles himself by taking on human flesh and being born of the Virgin. Our God is humble. And the mother of God is humble! For both Jesus and Mary, servanthood is central to their humility. Mary declares she's God's servant, and St. Paul says Jesus took the form of a slave. To become humble means we serve others.

St. Teresa of Calcutta, affectionately called Mother Teresa, exemplifies a humble servant of the Lord. She obeyed the prompting of God and started to care for the poorest of the poor. She nursed the wounds of people at whom the world would not even look. It takes great humility to serve in this way, because we have to say no to our own likes, desires, and interests, and yes to other challenging plans.

Humility corrects pride. Sometimes we might boast about the work we have accomplished or feel the need to tell someone about whatever it is we recently did. To be humble might mean we do not share everything about our lives. In the spiritual life we call this hiddenness. I like to consider it making small secrets with God—if we do something for another person, we do not need to boast about it and tell everyone; instead, it is a small act only God and you know about. It is for God's glory and not our own. We become humble when we act in this way.

In our age of social media, it is easy to vie for attention and recognition from our "friends" or "followers." It's really a form of pride. Looking to the example of Mary, we know what a humble heart is. We are called to become, like Jesus and Mary, servants to others, and when we do, it's then that we begin to form a humble heart.

Prayer to Mary Our Intercessor
Mary, my mother, give me a heart like yours, a humble heart that serves the Lord.

Today's Step toward Living with a Marian Heart
Try to do something kind for another person today. Do not tell anyone what you've done. Instead, lay it at Mary's feet as an offering for the salvation of souls. In this way, you give away the good of the action and keep it a secret between you, God, and the Blessed Mother.

Day Eight

A Heart That Bears Wrongs

Scripture

> *When his mother Mary had been engaged to Joseph, but before they lived together, she was found to be with child from the Holy Spirit. Her husband Joseph, being a righteous man and unwilling to expose her to public disgrace, planned to dismiss her quietly.*
> —Matthew 1:18–19

Reflection

During the Year of Mercy proclaimed by Pope Francis (December 2015 to November 2016), much attention was focused on the corporal and spiritual works of mercy. One of the spiritual works of mercy is to bear wrongs patiently, as Mary often did.

Many scholars believe Mary was a very young woman at the time of Jesus' birth—perhaps even a teenager. Think about it: a young woman, betrothed to a man named Joseph, goes off to visit her cousin Elizabeth miles away, stays there for three months, and returns home visibly pregnant. Ignatius Press's *Mary of Nazareth* provides one cinematic perspective on what may have occurred when Mary returned. Before Mary's departure, Joseph worked to build a home for the two of them, and when Mary returns she meets Joseph there. He sees her visibly pregnant. After this experience, Joseph tears down parts of the house, falls asleep on the property, and then receives his dream telling him to take Mary into his home. Later scenes of the film depict the wedding of Joseph and Mary. Music plays, but only a few dance. The silent spectators to the affair look on with judgmental glances at Mary, perceiving her to be an adulteress.

Mary said yes to being the mother of the Lord. And that yes came with a cost. People began to look at Mary with disdain. Joseph, the one she loved, wanted to quietly divorce her. Joachim and Anne, Mary's parents, might have believed Mary brought disgrace upon their family name. Mary's neighbors probably began to talk about her, saying unkind words. While all this was happening, the heart of Mary simply bore these wrongs patiently. Her faith and trust in God and the events that transpired at the annunciation assured her that all would work out for good. Soon the plan of God would unfold, Jesus would be born, and many would begin to realize the purpose of Jesus' birth.

In our own lives, people might say unkind words about us. And many times what they say may not even be true. As a Christian people, we are called to forgive the people who wrong us. Jesus tells us to pray for our persecutors and to do good to those who hate us. In essence, this is an invitation to bear wrongs patiently. Sometimes the wrongs we have to bear come as a result of faith. People might gossip about our practices of faith: they don't eat meat on Fridays, they have too many kids, and so on. Do not become angry. Do not allow them to take away the peace that is accorded to followers of Jesus. Bear the wrong, pray for their souls. Be like Mary.

Prayer to Mary Our Intercessor

Mary, my mother, give me a heart like yours, a heart that bears wrongs patiently. Help me to love everyone, even those who hurt me, and please intercede for me, that I may never say an unkind word about another person.

Today's Step toward Living with a Marian Heart

Is there someone in your life against whom you are holding a grudge? Ask God for the graces to forgive that person. When we are able to forgive, a great weight will be lifted off our shoulders.

Day Nine

A Heart That Adores

Scripture

> *And she gave birth to her firstborn son and wrapped him in bands of cloth, and laid him in a manger, because there was no place for them in the inn.*
>
> —Luke 2:7

Reflection

Parents are mesmerized by their firstborn and take great joy in showing their child to those around them. In a sense, they adore and marvel at their child as they gaze upon his or her face for the first time. Now, imagine the same adoration that comes forth from the heart of Mary, the Mother of God. Not only does she adore the face of her child but also she adores the face of the incarnate Son of God. Joseph and Mary are not the only ones who adore Jesus. In time, the three kings came to adore the Christ child and brought him their gifts.

Today, we as Catholics have the profound gift of being able to adore Jesus present in the Blessed Sacrament of the altar. We can adore Jesus hidden in the tabernacle, or, in some cases, exposed in a monstrance for an hour or perpetually in a chapel. Just as Mary stared at Jesus as he lay in the manger or in their home at Nazareth, we have the ability to stare at Jesus. When we go to adoration, we gaze at Jesus and allow him to gaze at us. Adoration changes lives and hearts. As we gaze upon Jesus, he can pierce the inner depths of our hearts, healing our wounds, purifying our minds and hearts of evil, and drawing us closer to himself. In the gospels, when the three kings left after adoring Jesus, they went home a different way. When our hearts are filled with adoration, we begin to change.

Not only do we have the ability to adore God himself but also we can adore God in his created works. Any person who has seen a picturesque scene at the mountains, a gorgeous sunset, or any other natural beauty surely has adored God for who he is. This is precisely what adoration is, adoring God for being God. In the grand cathedral of the outdoors, we can adore the Divine Architect who crafted the entire world.

When I visited Lourdes for the first time, adoration of God welled up within my soul. I was in wonder and awe at what God had done and accomplished at that place. I was caught up in the beauty of Mary. Her sinlessness allows her to be called the all-beautiful one. The grotto mesmerized me, especially how God transformed what was the town's garbage dump into a beautiful sanctuary of grace when Mary appeared there. Last, during my trip I encountered the beautiful manifestation of God's will. Everything on the trip went according to his design. My group consisted of me and three others: a friend, a dad, and a teenaged girl with cancer who had long desired to go to Lourdes. We were there for only two days, but God filled those days. On our arrival we went to the English Mass. Since I'm a priest, I concelebrated at the Eucharist. The celebrant shared who I was, where I was from, and why I was in Lourdes. After Mass, I met a few people from New York who were on pilgrimage seeking healing from cancer for one of their companions. I promised my prayers for them, and as we parted, I didn't think we would see them again. Later that night, we dined at a restaurant and happened upon those same pilgrims, whom we invited to join us at our table. The father in my group began to share why he and his daughter had come to Lourdes. He shared with the group from New York many of his drawings from the pilgrimage and other drawings he had done. As the conversation went on, he wanted to give a drawing of a butterfly to the woman from New York who was praying for a miracle. Little did he know that the butterfly was an image that held deep symbolic meaning for her, which she related to all of us. As the conversation continued throughout the night it became very clear that God was guiding our encounter and conversation. I was a spectator privileged to be a part of the conversation. I recall being caught up in the beauty of the moment, seeing how God was at work in this pilgrimage and how nothing was by coincidence. The entire experience led me into prayerful adoration, contemplating the plans and designs of God. After we finished dinner, we all went down to the Grotto of Massabielle where I anointed both cancer patients. In Lourdes Mary taught me what it meant to have a heart that adored God. All of my experiences led me to adore the omnipotent God.

If we have a Marian heart that adores, we can be caught up in the majesty of God. Like Mary, we can adore God in the flesh, as he comes to us in the Blessed Sacrament, or we can adore him in his creation. There are many moments for adoration; we simply need to find them and be attentive to them.

Prayer to Mary Our Intercessor

Mary, my mother, give me a heart like yours, a heart that adores God. Help me to marvel at the work of God and to adore him in his creation and in the Eucharist.

Today's Step toward Living with a Marian Heart
Take a few moments to adore God. You might do this by watching the sunset, taking a walk along a nature trail, or stopping by your local church.

Day Ten

A Heart Pierced by a Sword

Scripture

> *Then Simeon blessed them and said to his mother Mary, "This child is destined for the falling and the rising of many in Israel, and to be a sign that will be opposed so that the inner thoughts of many will be revealed—and a sword will pierce your own soul too."*
>
> —Luke 2:34–35

Reflection

Many devotional paintings depict Mary's heart pierced with seven swords, representative of the seven sorrows of Mary: the prophecy of Simeon, the flight into Egypt, the loss of Jesus in the Temple, the meeting of Jesus and Mary along the Way of the Cross, the Crucifixion, the taking down of Jesus from the Cross, and the burial of Jesus. These swords are metaphors for the pain that the Mother of God experienced.

There are many swords that can pierce the hearts of modern men and women today. Sometimes our own family may inflict the sword. There are many parents who see their children living immoral lives. Or their children have left the Church and no longer attend Mass, or their children's children might not be baptized. Concerned parents become overwhelmed with the state of their child's soul. It's like a sword piercing their hearts, because the way they raised their children does not correspond to the way their children go on to live their lives.

Other people might feel abandoned by their families, because no one helped them in their time of need. This could have been at the death of a loved one, a terrible sickness, or other troublesome circumstances. Lack of charity in families pierces like a sword.

Another sword piercing the hearts of many might be hurtful words that family, friends, or coworkers have flung at us. When people speak unkindly about us, it is a type of betrayal, piercing our hearts with a sword.

At times the sword of helplessness can pierce our soul—when we see a loved one suffering or dying or in other situations in our world that we see: abortion, war, terrorism, human trafficking, and so forth. All these things pierce our hearts with pain for other people as we sympathize with their plights.

Swords of sadness in our souls, caused by depression and anxiety, are moments in which our hearts are pierced.

If you have experienced the sorrows of this life, if your heart has been pierced in some way, do not give up or lose hope. Having a heart filled with sorrow shows the sensitivity of our souls and their closeness to God. Keep your faith and persevere. All these swords we experience leave wounds in our hearts that only God can heal. Healing can happen in this world, especially by way of the sacraments and personal prayer. Relief from suffering—from depression or anxiety, for example—can come in this world as well. Mary gives us an example of hope. One of her sorrows was death, but that sorrow was lifted when she received word that Jesus was alive.

If your heart has been pierced by a sword, that means there is a woundedness that causes you pain. Bring that hurt and pain to prayer. One common Marian prayer, which concludes the Dominican Rosary, is the Hail Holy Queen. At a time when my heart had been pierced by a sword, I was praying the words of that prayer. As I said, "To thee do we send up our sighs, mourning and weeping in this valley of tears," I realized that I was surrendering to her motherly intercession all my worries, all my hurts, and asking her to bring them to Jesus. Mary's heart experienced many of the things that fill our hearts with sorrow.

As we give our hearts to Mary, and in turn to Jesus, her heart becomes filled with sorrow for us, her children, as she sees our suffering, pain, and anguish. This leads her to pray for us.

In our spiritual journey through this book we are asking Mary to give us a heart like hers. When our hearts are afflicted with swords, we can identify with her. Ask her to intercede for you and seek the healing you may need for whatever swords have pierced your heart.

Prayer to Mary Our Intercessor

Mary, my mother, give me a heart like yours; when my heart is overcome with sorrow, give me strength to turn to God in faith.

Today's Step toward Living with a Marian Heart

Think about one of the swords of sorrow that has pierced your heart. Offer a prayer to God, asking him to heal whatever wounds you might have, and to give you strength and courage to persevere.

Day Eleven

A Heart That Ponders

Scripture

> *But Mary treasured all these words and pondered them in her heart.*
>
> —Luke 2:19

Reflection

The evangelist Luke tells us that the heart of Mary is one that ponders, or, in other translations, treasures the events of life in her heart. There are two instances in which Luke makes specific reference to Mary's heart: first in the Nativity account, and second, after the finding of Jesus in the temple. She pondered in her heart the visits from magi and kings, and the gifts her son received while in Bethlehem. The gospel does not tell us everything that happened after the birth of Jesus, so I am sure there is much more she pondered. In her heart she treasured the episode of Jesus among the elders in the temple and the words Jesus spoke to her. Knowing that Luke makes reference to Mary's pondering and keeping things in her heart, I am sure she treasured all the moments of Jesus' life, during those hidden years, his public ministry, and what followed thereafter.

Chiara Lubich, the founder of the Focolare Movement, also known as the Work of Mary, in her own prayer reflecting on how Jesus left his presence on earth in the Blessed Sacrament in all the tabernacles of the world, asked Jesus in prayer why he did not leave the presence of his mother in some way. In Chiara's own prayer, she came to realize that Jesus wished to see Mary mirrored in Chiara.

All throughout life we have opportunities to become like Mary by pondering and treasuring the events of our lives. This came true to me in a very poignant way. After I was ordained a priest, I celebrated my Mass of Thanksgiving at my home parish. For a communion meditation, a soloist sang Brian Flynn's "You Are a Priest Forever." The song had special importance to me because it was played at a dear priest friend's funeral a few years earlier. Sitting in the presider's chair, full of the day's emotions, I wept tears of joy and gratitude as I listened to the singer. The videographer who recorded the Mass lost some footage in a hardware malfunction; some of the lost footage included that very moving song. I was initially very disappointed, but over time I realized this was a moment for me to become like Mary, treasuring and pondering that event and what

I had experienced in my heart. When I want to relive that moment, I close my eyes, reenvision the scene, and allow it to come back to my memory.

In our lives there is much we can ponder and keep in our hearts: the joys of our childhood, momentous occasions, and the experiences we had with a loved one. Treasuring the memories of our deceased relatives and friends is a way that their memory lives on in our hearts. We all have formed many memories, both good and bad. Hopefully we can put away the bad, and ponder the good!

Prayer to Mary Our Intercessor

Mary, my mother, give me a heart like yours, a heart that ponders the events of my life. Help me to remember the past and be grateful for what has come my way.

Today's Step toward Living with a Marian Heart

Is there a certain person or event that meant a lot to you? Call to mind a positive, important, or meaningful memory and sit with it for a few minutes. Treasure the experience; relive it in your mind and heart; afterward give thanks to God for that person or experience you pondered.

Day Twelve

A Heart That Searches for God

Scripture

> *Now every year his parents went to Jerusalem for the festival of the Passover. And when he was twelve years old, they went up as usual for the festival. When the festival was ended and they started to return, the boy Jesus stayed behind in Jerusalem, but his parents did not know it. Assuming that he was in the group of travelers, they went a day's journey. Then they started to look for him among their relatives and friends. When they did not find him, they returned to Jerusalem to search for him. After three days they found him in the temple, sitting among the teachers.*
>
> —Luke 2:41–46

Reflection

The second person of the Blessed Trinity, Jesus Christ, became incarnate of the Virgin Mary and became man.

God dwelt among us. As one of my seminary professors used to say, "He lived our life, talked our talk, walked our walk, died our death, and rose to eternal life." Joseph and Mary enjoyed a unique relationship with God, because Jesus lived in their home.

Imagine what they must have thought when they lost the incarnate Son of God on their way home from Jerusalem. What did they do in response? They set out searching for God!

Today many people are searching for God. Their hearts are not satisfied. St. Augustine famously captured this when he said our hearts are restless until they rest in God. Some people, who do not know what they are looking for, turn to other things to fill the longing—overeating, alcohol, electronic media, and other addictions. Other people feel abandoned by God, and so they continually seek God's love anew.

During times of tragedy and crisis we might ask ourselves, "Where is God?" During terrorist attacks or medical crises we might feel abandoned by God or ask how God could allow such things to happen. Yet it is precisely in these moments people begin to search for God. The night of September 11, 2001, there probably was not an empty church in our country. People searched for God and fell on their knees in prayer. The same is true when a person is sick. Sometimes prayer vigils may be held, or a person might seek God through the sacrament of the Anointing of the Sick.

In secular society, where it seems that God has been erased, we might ask ourselves, "Where is God?" Bishop Robert Barron, in his book *Seeds of the Word: Finding God in the Culture*, attempts to find God in our lives today. Bishop Barron finds God and elements of faith in novels, movies, art, current events, politics, and the culture. He seeks to train each person to see God in the ordinary and the secular.

A heart like Mary's knows God and, when it doesn't perceive him nearby, goes in search of God. When God seems to be absent from your life, do a review of the present day or past week and try to recall those moments in which you were aware of God. This is called the practice of the presence of God. The truth is that God never abandons his people. We know where we can find Jesus in our lives today, reserved in the tabernacle in any Catholic Church. Sometimes finding Jesus is much easier than we expect, because he is exactly where he has promised to be. Mary found Jesus sitting among the teachers, right where she left him. Every time we attend Mass, he comes to stay under our roofs. If we think Jesus is not at our side, perhaps we need to seek him in his Father's house.

Prayer to Mary Our Intercessor

Mary, my mother, give me a heart like yours, a heart that searches for God and discovers joy in finding him.

Today's Step toward Living with a Marian Heart

Over the next few days, make a list of where you found God in your life. If you do a weekly holy hour of adoration, review the week, searching for those God moments.

Day Thirteen

A Heart That Listens to God

Scripture

> When his parents saw him they were astonished;
> and his mother said to him, "Child, why have you
> treated us like this? Look, your father and I have
> been searching for you in great anxiety." He said to
> them, "Why were you searching for me? Did you not
> know that I must be in my Father's house?" But they
> did not understand what he said to them. Then he
> went down with them and came to Nazareth, and
> was obedient to them. . . . And Jesus increased in wis-
> dom and in years, and in divine and human favor.
> —Luke 2:48–52

Reflection

Many people believe they do not hear the voice of God.
And they might be right. They probably have never audi-
bly heard the voice of God. Mary and Joseph could never
make such a claim. So unique was their experience, living and caring for the Son of God. For years they shared
privileged moments with Jesus, listening to his voice, and

hearing the wisdom he imparted. We are offered a unique snapshot into the Holy Family's conversations when Jesus' parents find him in the temple: Mary asks a question, and Jesus obliquely and cryptically responds! It's interesting to note that St. Luke tells us that after Jesus responded, Joseph and Mary did not understand what Jesus had said. Sometimes we might feel like Joseph and Mary: we've listened to God, we've heard him speak to us, but maybe it doesn't make sense. That's when we ask God for clarity and direction, spending even more time listening to God in prayer, allowing God to make clear the words he has spoken to us.

Even if we don't always feel it's true, God speaks to us today. He speaks in varied ways. One way that God speaks to us is through the sacred scriptures. Have you ever read the Word of God and known that a verse was meant for you and your circumstances? This can also happen with spiritual writers. For me, whenever I read the writings of Chiara Lubich, who founded the Focolare Movement, I always feel what she wrote was written just for me at that precise moment! I had a rough week once, and I had reached a breaking point. Not knowing where to turn, I went to a local adoration chapel in order to make sense of everything. I spent three hours there, praying and sorting through the recent events. I opened up a book by Chiara Lubich and read where I had left off several days prior, and the passage I found gave me much consolation. She wrote that if we believe God is with us and loves us in good moments, then we must also believe God is with us and loves us in the bad moments too. At that particular moment I needed to hear that God was with me, and Chiara Lubich's book spoke that word to me. I have had this happen so many times, that whatever struggle I am facing, whenever I pick up a book for spiritual reading, it addresses exactly what I need. To hear God's voice in this way we need to read scripture or do spiritual reading. If we think we are not hearing God's voice, it might be because we do not provide him the opportunity to speak.

God also speaks to us through other people. Many priests and religious report that they started thinking about their vocation because someone told them they would be a good priest or religious. God worked through that person to offer an initial invitation, and the receiver listened and prayed about it, listening for God to speak further. It is important to listen to those around us, because God may be speaking through them.

Lastly, if we become strongly convicted of something, and there is a stirring in our soul, God might also be speaking. Such an experience became very real for me on the feast of St. Thérèse of Lisieux. The trip to Lourdes that I made in January 2016 when I went there with a friend, a dad, and his daughter who had cancer was part of a larger journey to France: I needed to conduct research for a paper I would give at a conference later that year. The teenaged girl had been dreaming of going to Lourdes, and that happened to be my last stop. The four of us—the girl, her father, my friend, and I—set out on a pilgrimage to visit two basilicas in France dedicated to an obscure title of Mary that I was researching. Since we were in France, it only made sense to visit the various holy sites in that country, including Lisieux.

St. Thérèse lived in Lisieux and at a young age wanted to join the Carmelite monastery in the village. Thérèse recounts her life story in her autobiography-turned-spiritual-classic, *Story of a Soul*. Now, many people ask St. Thérèse's intercession, asking her to send them roses, because she promised, "After my death, I will let fall a shower of roses. I will spend my heaven doing good upon earth."

I've been devoted to St. Thérèse for many years. On her feast day in 2016 (October 1) I honored St. Thérèse by attending Holy Mass at the National Shrine of Mary, Help of Christians, in Hubertus, Wisconsin, run by Carmelite friars. At the end of Mass the main celebrant blessed roses to be given away to all in attendance. As I drove home, I thought of that young girl and her family, because her situation had worsened. I felt sure that the rose I received was meant for her. Since the family lived in the same town to which I was assigned, I called them on my way home and asked if I could stop by. Once I arrived, I gave the rose to the young girl and chatted with the family. About fifteen minutes after I arrived, the other person who journeyed with us to France, who lives an hour away, stopped by their house with a bouquet of roses. A reunion ensued!

In the depths of my heart I had heard God asking me to give that rose to the young girl. I could have reasoned I was too busy or I didn't have enough time. But I listened to God, and it became apparent, in the events that occurred, that I did what he wanted. One caveat regarding our listening for God's voice within: if what we become convicted of goes against morality or the teachings of the Church, there's a good chance it's not God's voice we are hearing. It is important to subject the promptings of the spirit to prayerful discernment, both by ourselves and also by other trusted spiritual leaders.

Mary can teach us many things about listening to God: First, we need to have time for silence. God cannot speak if we do all the talking. Second, give God time to speak. God can speak in the midst of our business, but God also speaks when we devote specific time to him. Find a place where the noise of the world fades away. It does not need to be a church. It can be anywhere: the beach, the woods, a nature preserve, or a prayer corner in our own homes. These are the places where we give God the opportunity to speak. Third, be aware of how God can speak—scripture, spiritual reading, or other people. Listening for the voice of God will create in us a greater awareness of God's will, leading us from prayer to action.

Prayer to Mary Our Intercessor

Mary, my mother, give me a heart like yours, a heart listening to the words of God. Help me to hear and live them in my life.

Today's Step toward Living with a Marian Heart

Turn off all your electronics (cell phone, tablets, computer, etc.), and sit in silence for five to ten minutes. Listen for God's voice deep within. What does he say to you? Try doing this every day, adding a minute more each day!

Day Fourteen

A Heart Attentive to Others

Scripture

When the wine gave out, the mother of Jesus said to him, "They have no wine."

—John 2:3

Reflection

A number of years ago, I discovered one of my now-favorite titles of Mary when I read Bl. Paul VI's 1974 apostolic exhortation *Marialis Cultus*. He called Mary the attentive Virgin. He does so in the context of describing Mary as one who received the word of God with faith. As I encountered that title, I could not help but associate it with Mary's attentiveness to the needs of others. This title fits in so many ways—attentiveness to Elizabeth and care for her, attentiveness to Jesus during those hidden years, and attentiveness to the need of the couple celebrating their wedding in Cana.

Have you ever had someone know you were having a bad day? Or someone knows something might have happened in your life, such as the loss of a loved one, because you seemed sad? This is an example of a person who has an attentive heart: he noticed something was different in your life because he knows you so well.

An attentive heart also sees where prayer is needed and makes intercession for others. Have you passed by an accident on the side of the road and said a prayer? Or heard news on the television and bowed your head in prayer?

One time while I was in Lourdes, France, I noticed a woman at adoration who seemed to be going through a rough time. She was slightly bent over, her head in her hands, and she breathed heavily. I did not know what she was experiencing and I did not ask her, but, realizing something was overwhelming her, I entrusted her in prayer to Our Lord and Blessed Lady, knowing that they knew what she needed.

Mary noticed the shortage of wine at Cana and then did something about it. She went to her son, Jesus, and made intercession, asking him to help them. Today, Mary continues to be attentive to our world from her throne in heaven, as she notices when the world needs a message calling us to conversion (think of her many apparitions). To have a Marian heart means we notice the needs of others and take action. It could be as simple as opening a door for a person whose hands are full or recognizing the

store clerk or barista as a unique person and calling him or
her by name. You could try to pay attention to significant
events in people's lives and send a text, e-mail, or letter
before the event, telling them you're thinking about them,
or send a message afterward, asking how everything went.
It takes attentiveness to do those things. The formation
of an attentive heart will help us to see God's presence
around us and recognize when others need help. It allows
us to reach out and be Jesus to another person or to let our
friends know that we are thinking of them and care about
them. Be attentive, and change someone's life. That's what
Mary did at Cana.

Prayer to Mary Our Intercessor

Mary, my mother, give me a heart that notices the needs
of others, an attentive and selfless heart.

Today's Step toward Living with a Marian Heart

Look for a chance to perform an act of kindness for someone. Consider doing this for someone you see on a regu-
lar basis; look carefully at the people around you—where
do you see a need? Where can you best show the love of
Christ? Be on the lookout for the right opportunity and
be attentive.

Day Fifteen

A Heart of Compassion

Scripture

Meanwhile, standing near the cross of Jesus were his mother, and his mother's sister, Mary the wife of Clopas, and Mary Magdalene.

—John 19:25

Reflection

The Latin roots of the word *compassion* mean "to suffer with." As Mary stood at the foot of the Cross, she suffered with her son in his Passion. I know mothers who have watched their children suffer pain and been present to them on their own Calvary as death drew near. These mothers would do anything to lessen the pain their son or daughter experiences. They truly suffer with their loved one.

Most days present the opportunity to suffer with someone. One way to suffer with a person is to accompany that person during a time of loss. Death can come at an unexpected moment. We all know people who have passed quite suddenly. When a loss is tragic, the mourners need comfort and support. They need people to carry them through these difficult times. I was present to one family in particular when they unexpectedly lost their husband and father. They were away on vacation when the husband experienced a sudden heart attack that ended up claiming his life. The family was inconsolable, and it was difficult for them to make peace with this sudden turn of events. What can you do to help someone in this situation? Suffer with the person and give whatever help you can. This family experienced the assistance of many strangers; many angels in our midst wanted to help them. The taxi driver refused payment; someone drove the family around the airport parking lot to find their vehicle. These simple actions spoke volumes to the family. People cared about them. And for a moment, these simple acts of kindness helped them to forget for a few seconds about the grief they were experiencing.

From the day I was ordained I have seen the struggles of many people. One night remains in my memory, when I attended a prayer gathering in the aftermath of a teenage suicide. The suffering of these young people was palpable. Everyone gathered that night to support one another, offering a shoulder to cry on and an ear to listen. When we support one another in moments of loss, we can lessen the loads people carry and, in some small way, suffer with others, taking on a small piece of their suffering ourselves.

Death does not present the only opportunity for a person to be compassionate. So many people today suffer with illnesses, temporary or terminal: cancer, heart disease, diabetes, depression. Maybe someone in our life is sick and suffering. Are there small ways to help them? Doing their grocery shopping, driving them to medical appointments, being present for a doctor's appointment? It takes a compassionate heart to journey with our family and friends in troubling medical times.

Besides death and sickness, there are other people on the streets who might pull at our heartstrings. When we see a poor person on the street, a homeless person begging, what goes through our mind and heart? Do we turn and look in a different direction or does our heart go out to that person? There may be very little we can do, at that moment, to help. Some people carry homeless care packages in their car with granola bars or socks. Maybe you will feel compelled to drop a few coins or bills in a poor man's hat, a homeless woman's cup. At the very least, offer a prayer for them, that they will find the help they need. These small actions allow us to suffer with these persons.

Pope Francis, in his papacy, has taught the Church to be more compassionate. Over and over again he talks about the art of accompaniment. When we accompany another person, we walk with her in her journey of faith, first listening to the other person and then responding. Pope Francis wants us to walk in the other person's shoes, and to provide slow and gentle guidance along the way. Sometimes the good that we want for another person, or even for ourselves, does not occur overnight but is a slow progression.

Mary showed compassion throughout her life. She traveled to the hill country of Judea and cared for her cousin Elizabeth. This act was compassionate and selfless, a giving of oneself in order to lessen the suffering of another. According to Venerable Mary Agreda's *Mystical City of God*, Mary often saw the plight of the other and would give what she had to that person. By her desire to alleviate another's suffering, Mary took on suffering herself. In your day-to-day life, how is God asking you to suffer with another person? Once you are able to answer this question, begin to live with a compassionate heart.

Prayer to Mary Our Intercessor

Mary, my mother, give me a heart like yours, a heart that suffers with others; give me a compassionate heart.

Today's Step toward Living with a Marian Heart
Whom does God want you to show compassion toward
right now? A sick family member? A friend? A neighbor?
How does God want you to accompany them? In what way
can you lessen their suffering? Pray about these questions,
and listen for God to speak.

Day Sixteen

A Heart That Loves All People

Scripture

When Jesus saw his mother and the disciple whom he loved standing beside her, he said to his mother, "Woman, here is your son." Then he said to the disciple, "Here is your mother." And from that hour the disciple took her into his own home.

—John 19:26–27

Reflection

Jesus shows his love for Mary from the Cross when he entrusts her to the care of John and vice versa. The Church sees John as a typological figure for the Church, meaning that, at the foot of the Cross, Mary becomes the mother of all believers. In virtue of this new office that she receives from Christ, she loves all her children with the heart of a mother.

There are beautiful images of Mary standing tall, with her mantle quite wide, embracing a broad group of people. This image of the people gathered under Mary's mantle captures the essence of Marian devotees—people from all ways of life. At one time there was a stigma associated with Marian devotion, specifically with the Rosary, that implied it was a devotion for the uneducated. The angelic psalter—or the Rosary, as we know it today—originally provided a way for the illiterate to join in the prayers of the monks who prayed the entire psalter, 150 psalms, each day. The 150 Hail Marys of the traditional three sets of mysteries represented the 150 psalms. But today, since the majority of the population can read and write, devotion to Mary is for everyone, rich or poor, saint or sinner.

In the Old Testament, God shows a special predilection for the *anawim*, or the poor. Mary proclaims this in her Magnificat when she says that God has cast down the mighty from their thrones and lifted up the lowly. Today, people from all different walks of life flock to the intercession of Mary. The sick make their appeal to Mary, whom they call on as the Health of the Sick. Many prisoners foster a devotion to Mary during their incarceration. The businessman who hits hard times seeks her intercession.

Mary loves all her children. When we struggle to love the people who cross our path, we should strive to imitate her heart. Is it easy to love the person who cuts us off in traffic or the person on the train who hasn't bathed in days? Can we look at the person who has some sort of visible imperfection, or do we turn away? God sends many people into our lives to love. We can say either yes or no. If we want to have the heart of Mary, we must say yes to the command of Jesus to love our neighbor and even our enemy.

Prayer to Mary Our Intercessor

Mary, my mother, give me a heart like yours, a heart that seeks to love all people. With your mighty foot, crush any evil in my heart that prevents me from loving all my brothers and sisters in Christ.

Today's Step toward Living with a Marian Heart

Think of some people in your life whom you find difficult to love. Ask God to remove whatever wound and bitterness there is, so that you might be able to love them sincerely.

Day Seventeen

A Heart Filled with Sorrow

Scripture

> *When Jesus had received the wine, he said, "It is*
> *finished." Then he bowed his head and gave up his*
> *spirit.*
>
> —John 19:30

Reflection

Many people are surprised to learn there are more types of Rosaries than the traditional Rosary most people pray. The Dominican Rosary, taught by St. Dominic, is the most traditional form: it contains the Joyful, Sorrowful, Glorious, and recently added Luminous Mysteries. The Franciscan Crown, with seven sets of mysteries, reflects on the joys of Mary, while the Servite Rosary, also known as the Seven Sorrows Rosary, leads a person through the seven sorrows of Mary: the prophecy of Simeon, the flight into Egypt, the loss of Jesus in the temple, the meeting of Jesus and Mary on the Way of the Cross, the Crucifixion, taking Jesus down from the Cross, and his burial. Devotion to the seven sorrows of Mary gained popularity during the twentieth century as a result of Mary's apparitions in the African town of Kibeho, Rwanda, where she requested the Seven Sorrows Rosary be prayed on Tuesdays.

When we pray the Seven Sorrows Rosary, we reflect on how Mary's heart mourned. After the birth of Jesus, Herod ordered that all the young infants be slaughtered, so the Holy Family fled into Egypt. As a mother, Mary's heart must have been filled with sorrow, knowing that the joy of parenthood was stripped from many parents on account of Jesus' birth. Mary's heart knew what it was to mourn for another person's loss.

There is a notable absence of Joseph in the scriptures after the finding of Jesus in the temple. John emphasizes that Jesus and Mary were at the wedding feast in Cana, but there is no mention of Joseph. Many scholars suggest Joseph died during the hidden years, but his death was not recorded in the pages of scripture. Many images depict the death of Joseph, with Mary and Jesus at his side. Mary's heart mourned the loss of her spouse.

Mary standing at the foot of the Cross also knew what it was to see the death of one's own child. Not only did she witness his death but also she saw him tortured and in agony, put to death in the cruelest of all manners. She stood there as a witness, overcome with the emotion of the moment; she endured mental anguish and physical suffering. No mother should have to watch her child die, take his last breath, and then have to bury him. Mary standing at the foot of the Cross knows what it is to mourn the loss of her son.

When someone we know is suffering health problems, it is as if this is his own passion, his own way of the cross. Those who stand by their loved one can look to Mary, first because during her life she knew that same sorrow, but also because, even now from her place in heaven, her heart is filled with sorrow for her children here on earth. As a heart filled with sorrow and grief was hers, so also it is ours when sickness and death strikes in our own life.

In our own grief and mourning, we can turn to Mary for help and inspiration. I cannot help but believe that as Mary stood at the foot of the Cross and heard Jesus utter his last phrases and saw him hand over his spirit to the Father, she maintained her faith that one day she would see her son again. She had spent many years with Jesus. She had heard him teach about life after death. I believe Mary knew she would be reunited with him; death would not have the final word, because Jesus would conquer the grave.

In 2010 my maternal grandmother, who had a hand in raising me, passed away. Though her death was expected, it was also, in some ways, unexpected. She went to the hospital for a sprained ankle, but during her stay her kidneys began to shut down, and death was imminent. What brought me comfort in this time of loss was my grandmother's devotion to Mary. She often prayed the Rosary, and as she prayed the Hail Mary over and over again, she asked Mary "to pray for us now and at the hour of our death." Those words are powerful: Mary, pray for me at the hour of my death. Even if a person prayed the Hail Mary only once in his life, I'm confident Mary remains faithful to that request. As a mother, Mary wants to comfort us in our times of sorrow.

Not only does Mary comfort us in our sorrow but also Jesus offers us consolation in his teaching that those who mourn will be comforted. In our grief, sorrow, and anguish God is there with us and has not abandoned us. One of the families with whom I journeyed through their loss of a loved one found comfort in a pocket coin they were given, which bore a quote from the popular Footprints poem. The back of the coin had these words etched on it: "It was then that I carried you." Those words were consoling. Looking back, they saw how Jesus, through the assistance they had received from others, had carried them.

We hear Psalm 23 at most funerals: "The Lord is my shepherd." In images of Jesus, the Good Shepherd, he carries a sheep on his shoulders. This is what Jesus does for us in our most difficult moments. He carries us. If your heart is filled with sorrow, ask Jesus to carry you through this time. As he carries you, listen to what he says to you: "I am here for you"; "I will help you through this." Allow your heart to be filled with faith and hope, replacing the sorrow of death and loss.

Prayer to Mary Our Intercessor
Mary, my mother, give me a heart like yours, a heart that mourns over death but rejoices in Jesus' promise of life after death.

Today's Step toward Living with a Marian Heart
Ask Mary today to wrap her mantle of love around the person or people you mourn. Ask her to share with them how much you love and miss them.

Day Eighteen

A Heart That Rejoices

Scripture

> *But he said to them, "Do not be alarmed; you are looking for Jesus of Nazareth, who was crucified. He has been raised; he is not here. Look, there is the place they laid him."*
>
> —Mark 16:6

Reflection

On Easter morning the Church begins to sing her Easter hymn to the Blessed Virgin, *Regina Coeli*: "Queen of Heaven, Rejoice, for he whom you merited to bear has risen as he said, pray for us to God, rejoice and be glad O Virgin Mary, for the Lord has truly risen!" Mary's heart knows what it means to rejoice, because her son, who once was dead, now is alive again. I can only imagine that Mary Magdalene, who stood with Mary at the foot of the Cross, announced this great joy to Mary of Nazareth and accompanied her to see the empty tomb. Some traditions even assert Mary of Nazareth was the first witness to the

Resurrection, staying at the tomb mourning and waiting. What joy Jesus' mother must have experienced when she discovered the empty tomb.

Luke, in his gospel, reports how Jesus raised the widow of Nain's son (see Lk 7:11–17). When Jesus happens upon the funeral procession, he is moved with pity toward the grieving mother. Marian scholars suggest Jesus took pity on this woman because he saw his own mother in her. Mary, a widow, would soon lose her own son to death. So, in an act of mercy, he restores life to this woman's son. In a way, this miraculous event foreshadows what happens on Easter morning, when Jesus, placed in the tomb for three days, rises from the dead. Life is restored. The widow of Nain had cause for much rejoicing, and likewise, Mary, who found herself in a similar situation, also rejoiced.

Mary's heart rejoices today when her children turn their lives around. At many shrines throughout the world, people come back to the Church, receiving God's mercy through the sacrament of Penance. Jesus said there is great rejoicing in the kingdom of heaven over one repentant sinner. Knowing that Mary shares in heavenly glory, we know that she too rejoices.

Mary experienced many sufferings in her life. She bore wrongs patiently, she fled into Egypt, and she saw her only son crucified as if he were a common criminal. After all these sufferings, there came a moment of resurrection, a day for rejoicing. In our own lives, there may be many Good Fridays, but we must trust that Easter Sunday will come and our sadness will be turned into joy.

There are many things that can cause us to become angry and sad. We have, in essence, two choices: we can walk around with a thundercloud over our heads always raining on someone's day, or we can try to find the sun emerging out of a storm. Jesus wants joy-filled disciples. Even in the midst of suffering, sadness, and pain, we must search for a reason to rejoice. If nothing else can bring us joy, knowing Jesus walks with us on our journey of life should bring us some sort of consolation. Mary's heart rejoiced in all the good things God had done for her; hopefully our hearts will be able to do the same.

Prayer to Mary Our Intercessor

Mary, my mother, give me a heart like yours, a heart that rejoices in the gift of each new day.

Today's Step toward Living with a Marian Heart

Reflect on what causes you sadness. Try to find the silver lining. Even in a bad situation try to find the good. When you discover it, you will have something in which to rejoice.

Day Nineteen

A Prayerful Heart

Scripture

> *All these were constantly devoting themselves to prayer, together with certain women, including Mary the mother of Jesus, as well as his brothers.*
>
> —Acts 1:14

Reflection

The Acts of the Apostles makes very clear Mary's presence among the disciples in the nascent Church because she joined them in prayer. After Jesus ascended to the Father, Mary finds herself among the disciples, in prayer, waiting for the promised Holy Spirit. Mary's life after Jesus' death surely was a life of prayer. In her role as mother of the disciples, she must have prayed for them as they went on their missionary efforts, knowing some would be martyred for their beliefs. I am sure she prayed for their safety, well-being, and for those to whom they evangelized. As Mary prayed, I imagine she continued to treasure the moments

of Jesus' life in her heart. She reflected on them. They were
a source of meditation for her.

When Mary appeared to Adele Brise, the Wisconsin
visionary, in 1859, she identified herself as the "Queen of
Heaven who prays for the conversion of sinners." Mary
identifies herself first in her role and second by what she
does. This title of Mary makes sense particularly in light
of the Queen Mother theology that Edward Sri and Scott
Hahn have proposed. The Old Testament depicts the queen
as the mother of the king. The queen mother would serve
as an advocate and intercessor for the people she represented. The people approached her with their problems,
and she would bring their concerns to the king. Mary, our
Queen, is our advocate today with her son, the King—she
is always willing to make intercession for us. In Champion, Wisconsin, Mary reveals her role as one who prays
for those on earth, specifically for sinners. Through this
private revelation, we can have confidence that Mary is
praying for us.

Many Catholics every day pray the Hail Mary. They
might pray it devotionally, as just one Hail Mary, or they
might pray three Hail Marys or the Angelus, or they
might recite the Rosary, which contains fifty-three Hail
Marys. Whenever we pray this prayer, we salute Mary in
the same way the angel Gabriel did and also in the words

of Elizabeth. In the second part of the Hail Mary, we ask Mary to pray for us, now and at the hour of our death. Those are powerful words as we ask Mary to remember us in prayer. Not only does Mary remember us in the moment in which we pray but also we ask her to attend to us when we draw our dying breath. Hers is the heart of a mother, a prayerful heart, always looking out for the needs of her children.

The prayerful heart of Mary is always ready to make intercession for us. Her intercession is shown in the Bible, for it was at the wedding banquet in Cana that Mary interceded for the couple. Today the Christian people invoke Mary under many titles, flying to her help and patronage, asking her to remember that anyone who fled to her protection would not be left unaided. People call upon Our Lady, Undoer of Knots, to untie the tangled knots of their lives. They ask Mary as Health of the Sick to obtain a cure and restoration of health. The faithful ask Mary to pray and intercede constantly for themselves, for others, and for the whole world.

Mary wants us to entrust our intercessions to her heart, because, with the love of mother, she will not forget our petitions and will intercede constantly on our behalf. Like Mary's, our hearts must become prayerful, attentive to those who need prayer, never forgetting those for whom we should pray. Do you have a prayerful heart? Learn from Mary how to pray by adoring and praising God and by interceding for others. This is the prayerful heart of Mary, and it should be our heart too.

Prayer to Mary Our Intercessor

Mary, my mother, give me a heart like yours, a prayerful heart. Help me faithfully lift my heart up to God in prayer each day.

Today's Step toward Living with a Marian Heart

Think of five people who could use your intercession today. Offer a prayer to God for them and their situations.

Day Twenty

A Heart Filled with the Holy Spirit

Scripture

> *By contrast, the fruit of the Spirit is love, joy, peace, patience, kindness, generosity, faithfulness, gentleness, and self-control. There is no law against such things.*
>
> —Galatians 5:22–23

Reflection

At the annunciation, Mary received the Holy Spirit in a powerful way, conceiving Jesus in her womb. This privilege allows Mary to be called spouse of the Holy Spirit. Whenever people receive the power of the Holy Spirit, they begin to manifest the Spirit's fruit, as outlined in St. Paul's letter to the Galatians—love, joy, peace, patience, kindness, goodness, faithfulness, gentleness, and self-control. Mary truly expressed love and kindness immediately after receiving the Holy Spirit when she went to serve her cousin

Elizabeth. Mary exudes joy as she proclaims the praises of God in her Magnificat. She was patient with those who disbelieved the miraculous happenings in her life.

The iconography and artistic paintings of our tradition always display Mary present at the Pentecost event. The Holy Spirit then descended for a second time upon Mary while she was in the Upper Room. (Some scholars suggest this would be the third coming of the Spirit in Mary's life, citing Jesus' last breath from the Cross as a sending of the Holy Spirit.) The coming of the Spirit into her life on Pentecost strengthened her for the remaining years she served God on this earth.

Like Mary, Catholics receive the power of the Holy Spirit, first on the day of their Baptism, and second, on the day of Confirmation. When was the last time you thought about the Holy Spirit and the gifts you received so many years ago? Do you remember the gifts of the Spirit? If not, here they are: wisdom, understanding, counsel, fortitude (or courage), knowledge, piety, and fear of the Lord. You first received these gifts at Baptism, and then they were strengthened and sealed on the day of Confirmation.

Imagine receiving a gift and never unwrapping it. I recently had this experience. I was decluttering my room, and I found a gift bag with a gift in it. I knew what was inside, a book, but I already had that book, so it had remained in the gift bag for several months. As I was cleaning up and organizing, I took the book out of the bag, only to find a card inside containing a gift of money. Do not let the gifts of the Holy Spirit remain an unopened gift. The next time you struggle to comprehend a situation and find God's will in it, ask for understanding. In a moment of weakness, ask for fortitude.

When we gain an awareness of how our hearts are filled with the Holy Spirit, it will change our lives and the lives of others. If our lives are filled with the Holy Spirit, we will begin to manifest the fruits of the Spirit. One night after I made my holy hour at a local adoration chapel, I decided to go to the movies. Immediately after an hour of prayer, I noticed a difference in my life, which was manifested at the theater. I was waiting in the concessions line (because you can't go to the movies and not get popcorn), and anyone who knows me knows how much I hate waiting in lines. (I have needed a patient heart from day one!) I was elated when the group ahead of me left the line. After a minute or two they got back in line and were behind me. As I approached the counter to order, I decided that the people behind me should go first. Their movie had already started; mine was starting in five minutes. I told the people behind me that they were in line first and should order. When I went to the soda fountain machine I reflected on what had just happened. I asked myself, "Why did I do that?" I realized the only reason I let those people go first was because I had just come from adoration, and God had changed my heart. I was manifesting the fruit of prayer, and, more importantly, the fruits of the Holy Spirit.

The Holy Spirit is the secret to a happy and fulfilling life—a life of love, joy, peace, and patience: the very things many people seek today. If we remain close to the Lord, and our hearts are filled with the Holy Spirit, people will begin to notice a difference; they will see that the Spirit has become our soul's most welcomed guest. *Come Holy Spirit, fill the hearts of your faithful, and enkindle in them the fire of your love, send forth your spirit, and we shall be created, and you shall renew the face of the world.* May this be true for you and for me.

Prayer to Mary Our Intercessor

Mary, my mother, give me a heart like yours, a heart filled with the Holy Spirit. Help me to live a life in the Spirit, living out the gifts I have received and manifesting the fruit of the Spirit each and every day.

Today's Step toward Living with a Marian Heart

Consider the gifts and fruits of the Holy Spirit. Which gift do you need most right now? What fruit do you want to live the most right now? Look for moments to ask the

Holy Spirit for the gift and for the opportunity to manifest the fruit.

Day Twenty-One

A Heart That Offers Counsel

Scripture

> *For a child has been born for us, a son given to us;*
> *authority rests upon his shoulders; and he is named*
> *Wonderful Counsellor, Mighty God, Everlasting*
> *Father, Prince of Peace.*
>
> —Isaiah 9:6

Reflection

Think of the despair the disciples felt in the aftermath of Jesus' death on the Cross. They left everything to follow this man. They abandoned their nets on the seashore and left their parents and families. For three years they followed Jesus and listened to his teachings, only to see him betrayed by one of his followers, arrested, beaten, and put to death like a common criminal. Even worse, these same followers abandoned Jesus at the foot of the Cross, save one—John the Evangelist. Peter, the leader of the apostles, even denied being his follower.

To whom would these disciples turn? I'd like to believe they turned to Mary, and both Mary and the disciples would mutually experience consolation. Maybe Mary reminded them of all the words and teachings of Jesus and provided hope that, after three days, he would rise from the dead.

The unique film *Full of Grace* captures the end of Mary's life. What struck me the most about this movie was Mary's relationship to the apostles and the early Church. Mary's spiritual motherhood of the apostles, and all believers, was very apparent. When Peter visited Mary, he shared with her the struggles he experienced in his debates in Jerusalem and his concerns about the unity of the Church. Mary simply listened and offered counsel. Just before Mary's dormition at the end of the movie, all the disciples gather together, and Mary imparts a farewell discourse.

Mary offered a listening ear to those who spoke with her. In fact, she still offers a listening ear today as our intercessor. Those who have doubts can talk to Mary as they would to their earthly mother and share their concerns and troubles. Mary, Undoer of Knots (to whom Pope Francis has a particular devotion), consoles and counsels the doubtful. The image was commissioned by a priest in gratitude for Our Lady's intervention in the doomed marriage of his relatives. The couple, who considered divorce, sought counsel from a priest, who took the ribbon used in the wedding ritual to unite the couple and untied knots within the ribbon. Thanks to Our Lady's intercession, the couple persevered in their marriage and overcame the difficulties they faced. Today many people who face doubts in their life, who have many knots, ask Our Lady to untie their knots just as she did for that couple many years ago. In a sense, you could say they turn to Mary for motherly counsel; she listens to their problems and returns counsel through the graces Jesus allows her to distribute to the world.

In our lives do we imitate Mary? Do we listen to others and offer counsel when necessary? Or when we spot someone we know, someone who will speak with us, do we run the other way, avoiding an opportunity for conversation? To have a heart that offers counsel means a person must be patient and willing to listen. Mary's heart, full of love and compassion and able to counsel the doubtful, becomes an example to us.

Prayer to Mary Our Intercessor
Mary, my mother, give me a heart like yours, a heart willing to listen and counsel the doubtful.

Today's Step toward Living with a Marian Heart
Give your full attention to the people you speak with today. Be attentive to the Spirit and offer counsel, if needed.

Part II

Desires of Mary's Heart

For the past twenty-one days, we have journeyed into the heart of Mary, discovering many attributes that the Mother of God possesses. Hopefully, as we seek to make our hearts more like hers—patient and compassionate, prayerful and filled with the Holy Spirit—we now look to the desires of her heart, and strive to adopt her desires as our own.

How have you been doing with your journey thus far? Have you noticed a difference in your life? Has your heart slowly been transformed? How are you doing with the daily action items? These are all good questions to ask as we begin the final ten days. If you have only halfheartedly meant the prayers you've prayed asking Mary to give you a heart like hers, I ask you now to recommit yourself to the last ten days. Prayerfully begin each meditation by asking Mary to obtain for you special graces, so that you will sincerely seek to have a heart like hers.

Day Twenty-Two
A Heart Desiring Unity

Scripture

> [Jesus said,] "I ask not only on behalf of these, but also on behalf of those who will believe in me through their word, that they may all be one. As you, Father, are in me and I am in you, may they also be in us, so that the world may believe that you have sent me."
> —John 17:20–21

Reflection

On the night Jesus was betrayed and handed over to his persecutors, he prayed for unity. If the disciples, while not asleep, overheard Jesus at prayer, I imagine they would have shared with Mary what he prayed for on the night before he died. If and when Mary heard this desire of Jesus, I am certain it would become an earnest desire of her heart.

Mary lived her life in constant union with Jesus. This unity began at the moment when the Holy Spirit came upon her, conceiving Jesus within her womb. In their home of Nazareth, the Holy Family sought unity in word and deed. In a powerful way, Mary, the compassionate one, was united with her son on Calvary as she stood beneath the Cross. We contemplate Jesus being placed in the arms of Mary during the Stations of the Cross. Mother and son, united again in that moment. After the Resurrection, Mary and Jesus were united once again for a time before he ascended into heaven. Unity was a hallmark of Mary's life.

After Jesus withdrew his bodily presence by ascending to heaven, the early Church still had the presence of Jesus every time they gathered and shared the Eucharist. The church at Corpus Christi Monastery in Rockford, Illinois, a Poor Clare Colettine monastery, houses a stained-glass window of Mary receiving the Eucharist. This is not a stretch of the imagination: given that John welcomed Mary into his home, she probably received the Eucharist as they remembered the night of the Last Supper, doing what Jesus commanded them to do—"do this in memory of me." Each time Mary received the bread, blessed and broken, transformed into the Body of Christ, she was united with her son, for he entered under her roof once again.

At the end of Mary's life, she desired to be united with her son once again. Jesus also desired this, so he raised her up into heaven, assuming her body and soul. There in heaven, Mary joins her son and lives eternally with him. Unity with God is our goal. We can experience a foretaste of this unity here and now through prayer and reception of the Eucharist. And one day, we hope to follow Jesus where he has gone before us, into heaven. There, like Mary, we will be united with him forever.

Mary desires unity, for this was the desire of her heart during her life. She desires for families to be united rather than divided. She desires unity in the Church. She desires her children to be united with Jesus through the Eucharist, as she makes apparent in her many apparitions emphasizing our reception of the Eucharist. In your life, seek moments of unity with God, for this is God's will and the desire of Mary's heart.

Prayer to Mary Our Intercessor

Mary, my mother, give me a heart like yours, a heart that desires unity. Help me always seek to be united rather than to cause disunity. By your prayers, may I one day achieve my soul's goal—unity with God forever in heaven.

Today's Step toward Living with a Marian Heart

The next time you receive the Eucharist, contemplate the unity Mary shared with her son and how you now share that same unity. After Holy Communion, close your eyes, and pour your heart out to Jesus, who has come under your roof. Share with Jesus your struggles and joys, and ask him to never allow you to be separated from him, that your will may always be united to his.

Day Twenty-Three

A Heart Desiring Our Salvation

Mary Speaks

> *Know for sure, my dearest, littlest, and youngest son,*
> *that I am the perfect and ever-Virgin Holy Mary,*
> *Mother of the God of truth through Whom every-*
> *thing lives, the Lord of all things near us, the Lord of*
> *Heaven and earth.*
> —Our Lady of Guadalupe to Juan Diego, 1531[1]

Reflection

Mary intervened in the evangelization of the Americas.
The work of the friars proved to be unsuccessful as they
gained few converts. Leave it to Our Lady to convert millions! When Our Lady appeared to Juan Diego, she did
so in the context of a culture that worshiped pagan gods,
even sacrificing their unborn. Craftily, Mary appeared as
one of them, in their native dress, using their symbols, to
tell them that she is the mother of the God of Truth, in
contradistinction to the false gods they worshiped. Mary
came to the people in Tepeyac because she desired their

salvation. Because of the words she spoke to Juan Diego and the miraculous imprint she left on his *tilma*, millions were converted!

Similarly, when Mary appeared to Adele Brise, the faith of the Belgian people was in crisis. Many of the immigrants who settled in northeastern Wisconsin were not accompanied by a priest. As a result, many stopped going to church and became lackadaisical in the practice of their faith. What happened? Mary appeared to Adele Brise, a twenty-eight-year-old immigrant, and asked her to gather the children in the wild country and teach them what they needed to know for salvation. In essence, the education of the children opened the possibility of their evangelizing their parents. The heart of Mary desires the salvation of souls.

Many of Mary's apparitions make reference to the sacraments of the Church: an encouragement to make a confession or receive the Eucharist regularly. The Queen of Heaven told Adele to offer her communion for the conversion of sinners and make a general confession. Mary directs us to the sacraments of the Church, because they are a means for our salvation. Jesus tells us that whoever eats his body and drinks his blood will have eternal life. Mary guides us back to the right path when we stray, because she wants us to love God and receive his love in return.

Like Mary, we too should desire the salvation of souls, beginning with our own, and then that of our family, friends, and the whole world. Some people have offered small sacrifices for the salvation of people's souls. In your life, maybe someone has told you "offer it up." In our lives, we can offer up our suffering for the salvation of souls. Some people invoke the Holy Family with a special prayer, "Jesus, Mary, and Joseph, I love you, save souls." In our own prayer we can show our concern for the salvation of souls. Then, maybe, the Spirit can use us to answer our own prayers. Perhaps you know someone who has fallen away from the practice of the faith. Reach out to them, and invite them to come to a church event or to Mass with you. In this way, you do what Mary has done: she gives an invitation and leaves it up to each person to respond.

Prayer to Mary Our Intercessor
Mary, my mother, give me a heart like yours, a heart desiring the salvation of souls. Help me cooperate in God's plan for the salvation of souls.

Today's Step toward Living with a Marian Heart
Offer a prayer today for those who do not know the love of God. Ask God to open their hearts so they may receive his

love in a powerful way. You might wish to pray the prayer the Angel of Portugal taught the children in Fatima[2]: *My God, I believe, I adore, I trust, and I love Thee! I ask pardon for those who do not believe, do not adore, do not trust and do not love Thee.*

Day Twenty-Four

A Heart Desiring
Our Conversion

Mary Speaks

I am the Queen of Heaven who prays for the conversion of sinners.
        —Our Lady to Adele Brise, October 9, 1859[3]

Reflection

A number of years ago, one of the readings from the Office of Readings struck me. The Office of Readings is one of the five daily prayers contained in the Liturgy of the Hours (Office of Readings, Morning Prayer, Daytime Prayer, Evening Prayer, and Night Prayer), which priests, deacons, and consecrated religious promise to pray each day. The reading for this particular Lenten day (Thursday of the First Week of Lent) came from quite an obscure saint, one whom I'm willing to bet you have never heard of: St. Asterius of Amasea.

He wrote:

Reflect for a moment on the wealth of God's kindness. Before he came as a man to be among men, he sent John the Baptist to preach repentance and lead men to practice it. John himself was preceded by the prophets, who were to teach the people to repent, to return to God and to amend their lives. Then Christ came himself, and with his own lips cried out: "Come to me, all you who labor and are over-burdened, and I will give you rest." How did he receive those who listened to his call? He readily forgave them their sins; he freed them instantly from all that troubled them. . . . What was the result? Those who had been God's ene-mies became his friends, those estranged from him became his sons, those who did not know him came to worship and love him.

After reading those sentences, I did precisely as St. Asterius instructed me to do—I reflected on the wealth of God's kindness. As I meditated, I could not help but realize a Marian connection. St. Asterius traces the historical lin-eage of our call to conversion from John the Baptist back to the prophets, and its renewal, through the preaching of Jesus. In fact, Jesus called people to conversion first in his preaching—"The time is fulfilled, and the kingdom of God has come near; repent, and believe in the good news"

(Mk 1:15). Besides the lector reading the scriptures and the homilist, who proclaims this message of conversion and repentance today? I'd like to suggest it's Mary. All throughout history, in Mary's many apparitions, she continues the same message of the prophets and John the Baptist and renews the call of her son Jesus.

When Mary appeared in 1531 to Juan Diego, she desired the Aztecs to believe in the one true God. Mary appeared in 1846 in La Salette, France, and emphasized keeping holy the Lord's day and not taking God's name in vain. In 1858 when she appeared to St. Bernadette, she expressed the need to pray for the conversion of sinners. One year later, in 1859, she gave the same message to Adele: Mary identified herself as the Queen of Heaven who prays for the conversion of sinners. Conversion is the earnest desire of Mary's heart. She wants us to follow the teachings of her son and to live the commandments. We often hear of statues or icons of Mary weeping. I do not wish to offer any endorsement of these phenomena—that's left to the local bishop—but why would Mary weep? Most likely it is on account of sinful humanity.

It is time for us to examine how we live our lives and to acknowledge the areas in which we need conversion. Maybe it's working through anger while we drive or curbing our sinful, gossiping tongue. When we convert our lives by turning them around and facing the Lord, we will please not only Jesus but also his Blessed Mother, who desires our conversion.

Prayer to Mary Our Intercessor

Mary, my mother, give me a heart like yours, a heart desiring conversion, not only that of the world but my own as well. Help me to find areas in my life where I am being called to change, and through your intercession obtain for me the strength to turn toward Jesus.

Today's Step toward Living with a Marian Heart

Find an examination of conscience, and thoroughly examine your conscience. Then find an opportunity to go to the sacrament of Penance. Conversion begins when we first acknowledge where we need God's help and then receive his mercy to begin again.

Day Twenty-Five

A Heart Desiring Pilgrimage

Mary Speaks

"Why do you come here?" asked one of the vision-aries. Mary answered: "So people come here on pilgrimage."
　　—Our Lady of Beauraing, December 23, 1932[4]

Reflection

On November 29, 1932, five children in the small village of Beauraing, Belgium, experienced the beginning of extraordinary events that would change their lives. Around six o'clock that night, the two Voisin children, Fernande (age fifteen) and Albert (age eleven) left their home in order to retrieve their sister Gilberte (age thirteen) from the local Catholic boarding school. The children passed by the Degeimbre home and decided to invite their friends Andrée (age fourteen) and Gilberte (age nine) to accompany them.

Once they arrived at the boarding school, Albert went to the door and rang the doorbell. Immediately as he turned around, he saw a woman suspended in the air above the railroad that was in close proximity to the school. His sister and friends also saw the same beautiful woman. The children recognized the woman as the Blessed Virgin and relayed what happened to Sister Valeria, who had opened the door; she did not believe the children. Gilberte Voisin, who did not know what the others had seen, walked out of the school and also saw the Blessed Virgin.

A similar appearance transpired again the following day, November 30, above the bridge, and likewise on December 1. However, during this apparition Mary relocated to a bush and then was seen underneath a hawthorn tree. Another thirty times, thirty-three in all, Mary appeared to these five children. She appeared wearing a long white dress with a long veil and with rays of light coming forth from her crown. On December 29, Mary revealed to the children her golden heart. Today many people refer to this apparition as Our Lady of the Golden Heart.

During a handful of the thirty-three apparitions, Mary spoke messages to the children. She told them to pray, pray very much, pray always. She also instructed the children to always be good. She identified herself under a variety of titles to the children—Immaculate Virgin, Mother of God, and Queen of Heaven—and described her mission, saying, "I will convert sinners." When asked why she appeared in Beauraing, Mary answered, "So people might come on pilgrimage." It is for this reason that Mary also requested a chapel to be built. The apparitions ended on January 3, 1933, when Mary parted with the words *Au Dieu*, signifying she would not return to Beauraing.

Mary revealed her golden heart to the children during these apparitions, and by her presence and the words she spoke she revealed another desire of her heart—that people might go on pilgrimage. Pilgrims set out to visit religious shrines, be they devotional shrines or places of apparition. Oftentimes people are drawn to places of apparition because of the reported phenomena that took place many years earlier. People go to Lourdes to seek healing and to bathe in the miraculous waters to which Mary directed St. Bernadette. Once Mary draws these people to her holy sites, she brings them to Jesus. Many pilgrims avail themselves of the sacrament of Penance after having been away from the sacrament for many years. They return to Mass and receive the Eucharist and then begin to foster a deeper prayer life. Mary leads pilgrims to Jesus.

Mary desires us to go on pilgrimage. A person need not go to Rome or Lourdes or Fatima. You can go on pilgrimage in your own backyard. There are many shrines dedicated to Mary and the saints throughout the world, and surely near where you live. Many times a pilgrimage requires sacrifice, in regard to cost and maybe less-than-ideal accommodations. This cost and inconvenience is a penance we take upon ourselves in order to draw closer to God. A pilgrimage reminds us that we are only pilgrims here on earth, journeying to the heavenly Jerusalem. Mary is the star guiding us, always leading us to her son. It's her desire that we go on pilgrimage, so let's get ready, and journey on.

Prayer to Mary Our Intercessor

Mary, my mother, give me a heart like yours; give me the desire to go on pilgrimage. As I journey through my life here on earth, help me remember that I am a passing guest on my way home to God.

Today's Step toward Living with a Marian Heart

Research the shrines in your geographic area. Look at your calendar and determine if it is possible to make a pilgrimage. If it is, begin preparing your heart by asking God to open your heart to receive the graces he wishes to give you at that holy site.

Day Twenty-Six
A Heart Desiring to Alleviate Suffering

Mary Speaks

I come to alleviate sufferings.
      —Our Lady of Banneux, February 11, 1933[5]

Reflection

Nearly a fortnight after the apparitions in Beauraing, which we learned about yesterday, Mary appeared again in Belgium, to an eleven-year-old girl named Mariette Beco. On January 15, 1933, Mary peered into the Beco family home.

Outside the window, Mariette saw a woman wearing a long white dress with a blue sash. The woman, barefoot, hovered over a cloud. Mariette's mother, disbelieving, jokingly suggested the possibility of it being the Blessed Virgin, who had appeared in Belgium only days earlier. Mariette persisted in her description of the beautiful, smiling woman who was in their backyard.

Mary again appeared to Mariette on January 18. The Blessed Virgin summoned Mariette outside. She ran toward her and followed Mary to a nearby spring of water, and Mary directed her: "Put your hands in the water! This fountain is reserved for me." On the following day, January 19, Mariette asked Mary for her name, after which she revealed she was the Virgin of the Poor. Afterward, Mary said, "This spring is reserved for all the nations, to bring comfort to the sick." In addition to other messages given, Mary requested a chapel built and many prayers offered. In Banneux, Mary revealed another desire of her heart—to alleviate suffering.

It is no coincidence that Mary spoke these words about alleviating suffering to Mariette Beco on February 11, the same day that Mary began appearing to St. Bernadette Soubirous seventy-five years earlier in Lourdes! Many people call Banneux "Little Lourdes" on account of the similarity of Mary's dress and blue sash, her desire to alleviate the suffering of the sick, and the connection to a spring of water. Between Lourdes and Banneux, Mary makes it apparent she wants to alleviate suffering and she desires healing, which happens in those places.

Many people go on pilgrimage to Lourdes in order to bathe in the *piscines* (pools). Lourdes is known as a haven for the sick, where people bring *les malades* (the sick) and allow them to be immersed in the healing waters. There have been cases of reported healings in Lourdes, where suffering truly was alleviated. But Lourdes is also a place where people find acceptance of their sickness and receive spiritual strength to continue their journey. People discover the peace they searched for, because Mary's heart desires to alleviate suffering. The hearts of some people also suffer the plague of unforgiveness. Through the power of the sacrament of Penance and the graces God gives, such suffering can be alleviated.

Thus far in our reflection for today we have focused on Mary's desire to relieve suffering, specifically ours, because we all experience suffering. It is good to focus on our suffering, because when we seek to relieve it and cope with it through the lens of faith, suffering can become redemptive, and offered for some intention. In these final ten days, we have been focusing on the desires of Mary's heart and asking that her desires might become our desires.

In this desire of Mary for the relief of suffering, we see the meeting of this desire with an earlier attribute, namely, Mary's compassionate heart. We learned that to be compassionate means to suffer with another person, and as we suffer with we try to help that person to the best of our ability. Hopefully you have had the opportunity to live with a compassionate heart. Now it is time to take that one step further and begin to alleviate the suffering of our family, friends, and strangers in whatever way possible.

The Litany of Loretto is a special litany of Marian titles asking Mary over and over again to pray for us. Mary is invoked under titles of Mother, Queen, and other titles from our Catholic tradition. One of those invocations comes to mind about Mary desiring to alleviate suffering. That title is "Consoler of the Afflicted." In Banneux and Lourdes, Mary consoles those who are afflicted with suffering, because she herself knew suffering while on earth.

Mary invites us to imitate her, to console those who are afflicted; she asks us to alleviate the sufferings of others. There is no scientific method that lays out how we can do this. Some people try to alleviate suffering with their checkbook by writing a check when they hear of some specific need. We see this especially when natural disasters hit or when someone from an agency for sponsoring a child speaks at Mass. Supporting charitable causes is only one way we can try to alleviate suffering. Another way some people feel called to help alleviate suffering is to do something about it themselves. One parish I worked at sponsored three or four different mission trips each year. One was a dental/medical mission trip, another was to a country in Central America, one was a mission trip in the United States, and there was also a youth mission trip during the summer. The people who went on mission trips actively sought to relieve the suffering of those to whom they were ministering. At a more local level, there are many opportunities to relieve suffering in your own hometown. Maybe there is a homeless shelter or a soup kitchen. Those who are homeless or poor know the suffering of being hungry. Consider signing up to donate a meal or to help serve a meal. Alleviate hunger by donating nonperishable items to the food pantry. Give away some of your excess clothing to the poor. These are simple ways that we can begin to live with a Marian heart, seeking to alleviate suffering throughout the world and even in our own backyard. You might know someone in your life who is going through a difficult time. Maybe someone you know recently lost a loved one and is alone. Give them a call or visit them. Or maybe you know someone who is struggling to make ends meet. As you prepare dinner one night, make a second batch and offer to bring it to them. These are just a few simple suggestions of how to alleviate suffering.

It's normal for us to want Mary to alleviate our sufferings. She has showed us that this is her desire, and we can ask her to do so when we call upon her intercession. But the greater prayer might be to ask God to give us the graces to help others in their time of suffering. When we do that, we transition from focusing on ourselves to looking outward to the needs of others. This is what Mary desired to do: bring comfort and relief to others. As she does that for us and for so many, we are then asked to make this desire of hers ours, and to live it in our lives.

Prayer to Mary Our Intercessor

Mary, my mother, your heart desires to alleviate suffering. Help me first to offer my suffering to the Lord so I may find peace from what afflicts me. Then help me see the sufferings of others and give me the desire to alleviate that suffering just as you desire to alleviate it yourself.

Today's Step toward Living with a Marian Heart

Given the twofold nature of today's reflection, first identify an area in your life where you need healing. Maybe it's family wounds, the inability to forgive, or an illness. Ask Jesus, through the powerful intercession of Mary, to lighten your load and alleviate your suffering. Then ask yourself, "How am I being called to alleviate the suffering of others? Who am I supposed to help?" I'd encourage you to bring this to prayer and ask God to open your eyes to those who are in need and give you the grace to respond to his prompting in your heart.

Day Twenty-Seven

A Heart Desiring Us to Pray

Mary Speaks

> *Pray. Pray Much. Pray Always.*
> —Our Lady of Beauraing,
> December 30, 1932, and January 1, 1933[6]

Reflection

Over and over again, when Mary appears, she encourages people to pray. In Lourdes, Mary told St. Bernadette to pray for sinners. In Champion, Wisconsin, Mary instructed Adele to pray for the conversion of sinners by receiving Holy Communion and offering her communion for that intention. In Fatima, Mary encouraged the children to pray the Rosary every day and to pray for sinners. The simple apparitions of Our Lady to the children in Belgium, both in Beauraing and Banneux, emphasized the necessity of praying. This common message reveals another desire of her heart: she desires us to pray.

It only makes sense that Mary wants her children to pray, because when we do so, we foster a relationship with her son. People of faith know they should pray. And perhaps they pray in very small ways—prayer before meals or a short prayer before bed. These are good starting points, but prayer is meant to be a relationship with Jesus. Do you pray daily? Are you satisfied with your prayer life? Or could it be better?

One of the biggest struggles people have with prayer is finding time. In the gospels, it often says Jesus woke up early and went to a deserted place to pray (see Mk 1:35). I think this is a good model for our prayer. It allows us to start our day off the right way by speaking and listening to God. If we put off our time for prayer to later in the day, it is possible other things will demand our time, and by day's end we have not spent any time in prayer.

Jesus also provides an example of where to pray. When the gospels tell us Jesus prayed, it often says he went off to a deserted place. Some people like to dedicate a particular area of their house to prayer and reflection by displaying religious images. For others, it may be easier to pray in a church or adoration chapel. And for others, the outdoors provides an opportune place to pray. The important thing is to find a place in which you are comfortable praying and then begin to make use of it.

With your prayer area determined, figure out how you would like to pray. Our Catholic tradition is filled with a variety of prayer styles and methods. There is no shortage of books on how to pray. In my own experience of prayer, I have identified three different types of prayer I try to engage in daily: liturgical, devotional, and personal.

Going to Mass is the highest form of prayer, because it is the prayer of the Church and a participation in the liturgy of heaven. It is a prayer that praises God, makes intercession, and offers thanksgiving. The Liturgy of the Hours is another form of liturgical prayer, prayed daily by priests and consecrated religious and also by the lay faithful. Consider learning how to pray Morning and Evening Prayer. In years past one needed to figure out how to use the complicated volume of Christian Prayer or the four-volume Breviary. In our technological age, the Liturgy of the Hours is available in apps for smart phones and tablets.

Many Catholics foster a devotion to the Blessed Mother or the saints. Most often devotional prayer is very formulaic, with certain methods or prescribed prayers. The most well-known devotion to Mary would be the Rosary, a set of prayers in which a person reflects on the life of Jesus. Another type of devotional prayer comes from apparitions of Jesus to St. Margaret Mary Alacoque and St. Faustina Kowalska. In the late 1600s Jesus revealed his Sacred Heart to St. Margaret Mary, and in the 1900s the polish nun St. Faustina received messages pertaining to the Divine Mercy. Devotions to the Sacred Heart of Jesus and to Divine Mercy emerge with each respective apparition. Devotion to the saints constitutes another aspect of devotional prayer, in which people recite prayers asking a saint to intercede for them. Commonly people pray novenas (nine days of prayer) to a saint for a particular intention. Some of the more popular saints include St. Jude, St. Pio of Pietrelcina, and St. Thérèse of Lisieux.

While devotional prayer could be considered personal prayer, I make a distinction, because, for me, personal prayer is giving God time to speak. One common form of personal prayer would be praying with the scriptures through lectio divina, in which a person first reads a passage of scripture, then finds a word or phrase to meditate on, then offers a prayer to God, and finally remains with God in a state of contemplation. St. Teresa of Avila taught the prayer of recollection, or mental prayer: the fostering of a stillness, listening to God in quiet. St. Ignatius of Loyola taught imaginative prayer, by which a person places himself in a biblical scene. There are many different types of prayer. Explore the methods and find one that best fits you.

Daily prayer is essential in the life of a Christian because it is the way we communicate with God. When we pray, we speak to God and God speaks to us. In our moments of prayer, we can try to make sense out of whatever is happening in our lives and discern God's will. Through our prayer, God gives us time for peace and quiet in our busy days. Prayer changes everything. It opens our hearts to the will of God and expands our hearts to love those for whom we pray. Perhaps this is why Mary desires us to pray—she knows it is for our good!

Prayer to Mary Our Intercessor

Mary, my mother, give me a greater desire to pray and seek union with God. Help me to find the time, the place, and the way I should pray each day.

Today's Step toward Living with a Marian Heart

Review the past week. Have you prayed every day? Do you find your prayer fulfilling? Set a prayer goal for the next week. Maybe it will be to spend ten minutes each day reflecting on the scriptures or looking for and trying out a new prayer method.

Day Twenty-Eight

A Heart Desiring Peace

Mary Speaks

Pray the Rosary every day, in order to obtain peace for the world, and the end of the war.
                    —Our Lady of Fatima, May 13, 1917[7]

Reflection

In two recent apparitions of Our Lady, the message she spoke made apparent her desire for peace. In Fatima, Mary requested that people pray the Rosary as a means to end the war. But the message of peace intensified during the July apparitions when Mary said, "You have seen hell where the souls of poor sinners go. To save them, God wishes to establish in the world devotion to my Immaculate Heart. If what I say to you is done, many souls will be saved and there will be peace. The war is going to end; but if people do not cease offending God, a worse one will break out during the pontificate of Pius XI." In essence, the apparitions of Mary to the three shepherd children of Fatima warned the world about pending unrest which could be averted through prayer and conversion. These two other desires of Mary's heart are in union with her desire for peace, for prayer and conversion can bring peace to the world.

Mary revealed a similar desire for peace in the village of Kibeho in Rwanda. During one of her apparitions, in August 1982, Mary allowed a teenage girl, Alphonsine Mumureke, to see a vision of the future. What she saw startled her: a river of blood, people killing one another, abandoned corpses, and cities in ruin. This prophetic vision was realized as the Rwandan genocide, which began in 1994. The apparitions of Mary in Kibeho served as a warning that if people did not convert and turn back to God, they might be deprived of peace.

There is a lack of peace in our world today. Many families are broken by division. There is senseless violence on our streets. Shootings occur now with greater frequency. Terrorists threaten to take away peace in our everyday life by their continued attacks.

We must work to bring about Mary's desire for peace in our world today. The prayer attributed to St. Francis asks the Lord to make us instruments of his peace. Is there division in your family? Strive to establish peace. Is there unrest in your place of work? Find ways to resolve the conflict. Does the threat to world peace bother you? Heed the message of Our Lady of Fatima and pray the Rosary for peace in the world. Peace can be attained only if we begin to desire peace and work to establish peace ourselves. The words of the song "Let There Be Peace on Earth" are true: *Let it begin with me!*

Prayer to Mary Our Intercessor

Mary, my mother, give me a heart like yours, a heart desiring peace. Help me to become a peacemaker in my family, workplace, community, and world.

Today's Step toward Living with a Marian Heart

Pray St. Francis's Prayer for Peace:

> Lord, make me an instrument of Your peace. Where there is hatred, let me sow love; where there is injury, pardon; where there is doubt, faith; where there is despair, hope; where there is darkness, light; where there is sadness, joy.
>
> O, Divine Master, grant that I may not so much seek to be consoled as to console; to be understood as to understand; to be loved as to love. For it is in giving that we receive; it is in pardoning that we are pardoned; it is in dying that we are born again to eternal life.

Day Twenty-Nine

A Heart Desiring Reparation

Mary Speaks

> *Sacrifice yourselves for sinners, and say many*
> *times, especially whenever you make some sacrifice:*
> *O Jesus, it is for love of You, for the conversion of*
> *sinners, and in reparation for the sins committed*
> *against the Immaculate Heart of Mary.*
>   —Our Lady of Fatima, July 13, 1917[8]

Reflection

In the 1600s, Jesus appeared to St. Margaret Mary Alacoque requesting the observance of the First Friday devotion
in honor of the Sacred Heart of Jesus in reparation for the
sins of humanity. In 1917, Mary appeared to Lucia dos
Santos and her cousins; Lucia later entered the convent and
received more aparitions in 1925. While the 1917 apparitions were approved by the Church, the other apparitions
never received such approbation. When Mary appeared to
Sr. Lucia again, she requested the observance of the Five

First Saturdays as a way to make reparation for the sins against her Immaculate Heart.

Why five first Saturdays? This was explained to Sr. Lucia in a later revelation from Jesus in 1930. The five first Saturdays were meant to make reparation for five different types of offenses against Mary's Immaculate Heart: blasphemies against the Immaculate Conception; blasphemies against her virginity; blasphemies against her divine motherhood and the refusal to accept her as the mother of humankind; the actions of those who attempt to instill in the hearts of children indifference, contempt, or even hatred of her Immaculate Heart; and the actions of those who insult her directly in her venerated statues and images.[9] To observe the five first Saturdays as an effort to make reparation, one must do specific acts. Our Lady outlined them during her apparition to Sr. Lucia on December 10, 1925: go to confession, receive Holy Communion, pray five decades of the Rosary, and keep Mary company for fifteen minutes while meditating on the fifteen mysteries of the Rosary.

At some point in your life you have probably offended someone by your words or actions. Sometimes, if we say something we should not have, we will try to immediately backtrack, hoping to fix our mistake. If we have hurt a person, we make attempts to apologize to her, trying to make everything right in our relationship. The same is true for our relationship with God. Sin offends God. By our acts of reparation, we tell God that we are sorry for offending him and will try our best to never offend him again. We also strive to make reparation for the sins of others who will not make such reparation.

In Fatima, Mary requested reparation to her Immaculate Heart not only because sin offends her heart but also because some people do not honor her with the respect and dignity she is owed as the mother of God. Mary desires for us to make reparation. It's the least we can offer to our God and his Blessed Mother for the offenses of our world.

Prayer to Mary Our Intercessor

Mary, my mother, give me a heart like yours, help me desire to make reparation for my sins, the sins of my family, and those of the whole world.

Today's Step toward Living with a Marian Heart

Reflect on the ways in which your sins or those of the world as a whole have inflicted pain on Jesus and Mary. With those images in mind, pray the following Act of Reparation to the Immaculate Heart of Mary:

> O Most Holy Virgin, our mother, we listen
> with grief to the complaints of your Immacu-
> late Heart surrounded with the thorns placed

therein at every moment by the blasphemies and ingratitude of ungrateful humanity. We are moved by the ardent desire of loving you as our mother and of promising a true devotion to your Immaculate Heart. We therefore kneel before you to manifest the sorrow we feel for the grievances that people cause you, and to atone by our prayers and sacrifices for the offenses with which they return your love. Obtain for them and for us the pardon of so many sins. Hasten the conversion of sinners that they may love Jesus Christ and cease to offend the Lord, already so much offended. Turn your eyes of mercy toward us, that we may love God with all our heart on earth and enjoy him forever in heaven.

Day Thirty

A Heart Desiring Obedience

Mary Speaks

Do whatever he tells you.

—John 2:5

Reflection

At Cana we noticed the attentiveness of Mary's heart. This event also leads us to discover a desire of Mary's heart—obedience. After declaring the shortage of wine and listening to Jesus' response about his hour not being at hand, Mary directs the servants to do whatever Jesus tells them to do.

Mary can exhort us to be obedient, because she first provided the example of one who was obedient. This obedience was evident at the annunciation when Mary rendered her fiat. She heard the plan of God and cooperated in the work of redemption. She revealed herself as the obedient daughter of Israel and as the New Eve.

Even Jesus spoke of Mary's obedience: "A woman in the crowd raised her voice and said to him, 'Blessed is the womb that bore you, and the breasts that you sucked!' But he said, 'Blessed rather are those who hear the word of God and keep it'" (Lk 11:27–28). Some people view this as a lack of respect for Mary, but a closer reading reveals Jesus' praise for his mother. Instead of thinking of the earthly, Jesus focuses on what will endure, in this case hearing the word of God and keeping it. As we reflected earlier during this journey into Mary's heart, she did hear the word of God, first through the angel and then as she listened to every word that came forth from Jesus' mouth. She obediently listened to these words, and further, kept them in her heart, as she often reflected and treasured these moments with Jesus. In a similar yet different account in Mark's gospel, Jesus says, "'Who are my mother and my brothers?' And looking at those who sat around him, he said, 'Here are my mother and my brothers! Whoever does the will of God is my brother and sister and mother'" (Mk 3:33–35). We know that Mary sought to do the will of God in her life, and thus she must be accorded as Jesus' mother, not only physically, but also in this spiritual sense as a doer of the word.

Anyone who reads the account of Jesus' Crucifixion in John 19 need only remember the exhortation Mary gave in Cana—*Do whatever he tells you*. From the Cross Jesus speaks to those gathered below: John (the Beloved

Disciple), Mary the mother of the Lord, Mary Magdalene, and Mary of Clopas. In the final moments of his life, Jesus entrusts his mother Mary to John and John to Mary. Our Catholic tradition has always seen John as representative of the people of God, the Church. When Jesus utters those final words, his last will and testament, he wants Mary to become the mother of all people. This is why we foster a love for the mother of God, because Jesus told us to do so. With an obedient heart, we do whatever Jesus has told us, and this is what he wanted us to do, to take Mary into our own home.

We see the convergence of many attributes of Mary's heart as we reflect on Mary's desire for obedience. We must search for God and find him in order to be obedient, which leads us to listen to God. The word "obedience" means to give ear or to listen. When our hearts search for God and listen to him, we are prompted to obey the words of God. As we listen, our hearts will say yes to what God asks.

We hear the words of God throughout scripture. We have heard the commandments given to Moses and we know Jesus' commandments to love God, our neighbor, and even our enemy. We hear him tell us that we must forgive others in order to receive forgiveness ourselves. We hear him tell us to feed the hungry and clothe the naked. We hear him telling us to behold our mother. And we hear him tell us to teach all nations. God has spoken. Are we listening? Are we obedient? Will we say yes?

Prayer to Mary Our Intercessor

Mary, my mother, help me to be always obedient to your Son and to the commands of God. Make my heart desire what your heart desires.

Today's Step toward Living with a Marian Heart

What command or teaching of Jesus do you find most difficult to live? Is there a way to embrace it and be obedient to Jesus' word? Create one plan of action to follow God's words more closely.

Day Thirty-One

A Heart Desiring Consecration

Mary Speaks

I shall come to ask for the consecration of Russia to my Immaculate Heart.
— Our Lady of Fatima, July 13, 1917[10]

The moment has come in which God asks the Holy Father, in union with all the Bishops in the world, to make the consecration of Russia to my Immaculate Heart, promising to save it by this means. There are so many souls whom the Justice of God condemns for sins committed against me, that I have come to ask reparation: sacrifice yourself for this intention and pray.
— Our Lady to Sr. Lucia, June 13, 1929

Reflection

The heart of Mary desires consecration. In Fatima, she specifically requested the consecration of Russia to the

Immaculate Heart. To be consecrated means to be set apart. Mary, herself, is a perfect example of one who was consecrated to God, because she was set apart for the specific purpose of being the mother of God.

When we consecrate ourselves to the Immaculate Heart of Mary, we set ourselves apart as children of Mary who look to her for an example and ask for her maternal solicitude and protection. A heart consecrated to Mary seeks to imitate the virtues of her life. In essence, they desire to have a heart like hers.

When I first received the inspiration to write this thirty-one-day journey into the heart of Mary, I never intended for it to be a preparation for Marian consecration. I shared the reflections as I wrote them with a friend and asked for feedback. After reading the initial draft of this book she commented to me that this book was a form of preparation for consecration to Mary's Immaculate Heart. If you believe this book has prepared you to have a heart like Mary's, I'd invite you to pray one of the consecration prayers found in appendix two of this book. By consecrating our hearts to Mary, we ask her to give us a heart like hers, so that we might live and love as she did and still does from heaven today.

More than anything, I thought this book would whet the appetite of a person who seeks to foster a deeper

Marian devotion; it is thus an entry into a form of total consecration to Jesus through Mary. It's possible that, as you began this journey, you were neither ready nor prepared for the idea of consecrating yourself to Mary. Maybe, as I initially hoped, this book has served as a gateway, opening in you a desire to prepare for Marian consecration. I would invite you to consider the forms of preparation for Marian consecration offered in appendix two.

Mary desires consecration. She desired the consecration of Russia. Additionally, as seen throughout the centuries and made known by spiritual masters, she desires our consecration. Consecrate yourself when the time is right. When you do so, you will become totally hers, and, in the end, you will have a heart like Mary's.

Prayer to Mary Our Intercessor

Mary, my mother, give me a heart like yours, help me to consecrate all that I do to God and your Immaculate Heart.

Today's Step toward Living with a Marian Heart

Have you consecrated yourself to the Blessed Mother? If not, is your devotion to Mary at a point that you could accept Mary as your mother and intercessor through a consecration to Jesus through Mary? Give some thought to whether you are ready to begin this process of total consecration. What Marian feast day would you choose? When would you start? Which method would you use?

Conclusion

In the end my Immaculate Heart will triumph!
    —Our Lady of Fatima, July 13, 1917

I t is by no accident that this book, *A Heart Like Mary's*, was published during the hundredth anniversary of the apparitions of Our Lady in Fatima. During the apparitions received by the three shepherd children, Mary revealed her Immaculate Heart. As we saw in the final ten days of our journey into the heart of Mary, at Fatima, Mary made known many desires of her heart: conversion, peace, reparation, and consecration. Mary also prophesied that in the end her Immaculate Heart would triumph. As we celebrate the centennial anniversary, and in the years that follow, we have an opportunity to allow Mary's Immaculate Heart to triumph through us. When we begin to manifest a heart like hers—a patient and generous heart, a listening and attentive heart, a heart that desires unity and peace— her heart triumphs over an impatient, selfish, disengaged, inattentive, fragmented, and troubled world.

During this journey, you might have found a few attributes or desires that you already possess. You also might have been introduced to other aspects of Mary's heart that you need to work to obtain. Pick one or two attributes or desires and focus on them. I also would encourage you to write your own prayer modeled on the daily prayers we have prayed throughout the past thirty-one days, asking Mary to help you obtain those specific attributes. Here's an example: *Mary, my mother, give me a heart like yours, an attentive heart, a chaste heart, a loving heart, a heart making intercession for others. Give me a heart like yours, so that I might love Jesus as you loved him.*

Our journey into the heart of Mary does not stop after these initial thirty-one days, because we now strive to live with her heart. After all, to live with her heart is to fulfill the mystical prayer of Chiara Lubich we learned about on Day Eleven—now Jesus sees his mother in us. Let Jesus see the heart of Mary in you by the way you live your life. Every day look for an opportunity to be Mary in the world, to love as she loved, to be humble as she was, and to go in haste and serve those you meet.

Acknowledgments

I would like to thank Mary Anne Urlakis, who graciously read the initial drafts and provided many suggestions. Thanks also to Mike Stark, the creator of Truth and Life Audio Bible, whom I am happy to call a friend and whose invitation to attend the Catholic Marketing Network conference allowed me to find a publisher for this book. I am indebted to Fr. Donald Calloway, M.I.C., who referred me to Michelle Buckman, a copy/line editor who assisted in bringing a final version forward to the publisher. Her suggestions in content were invaluable. I am grateful to my coworkers and parishioners at St. Raphael the Archangel Parish (Oshkosh, Wisconsin) who served as a sounding board for some reflections. And finally, to the baristas who helped me by their kind service at local coffee shops—thank you! My best writing comes when I withdraw myself from familiar environments and thus avoid distractions in my work or home office. The service of baristas was vital to this book!

Suggested Resources for Marian Consecration Preparation

Fr. Michael Gaitley, M.I.C. *33 Days to Morning Glory: A Do-It-Yourself Retreat in Preparation for Marian Consecration*. Stockbridge, MA: Marian Press, 2011. Fr. Gaitley provides a very straightforward and practical method of consecration by reflecting on the lives of four saints in very down-to-earth language.

St. Louis de Montfort. *True Devotion to Mary with Preparation for Total Consecration*. St. Louis de Montfort provides one of the original forms of Marian consecration. I often describe this method as a prayer marathon, because each day requires certain prayers to be recited. Some people find the language (e.g., "slaves of Mary") difficult. We must remember that St. Louis de Montfort wrote in a different time period.

Fr. Hugh Gillespie, S.M.M. *Preparation for Total Consecration according to St. Louis de Montfort*. Bay Shore, NY:

Montfort Publications, 2011. This is a more contemporary version of Marian consecration in the spirit of St. Louis de Montfort. Written by a Montfortian priest, the book serves as an introduction to the spirituality of St. Louis de Montfort and a method of consecration to Jesus through Mary.

Brian McMaster. *Totus Tuus: A Consecration to Jesus through Mary with Blessed John Paul II*. Huntington, IN: Our Sunday Visitor, 2013. Everyone knows of John Paul II's devotion to Mary. After the death of his mother, he knelt before a statue of Mary in his parish church and told Mary that she must be his mother now! He was so deeply affected by the writings of St. Louis de Montfort and Montfort's method of Marian consecration that he took the phrase *Totus Tuus* as his papal motto. Fr. McMaster weaves together the spirituality of St. Louis de Montfort and the writings of St. John Paul II for a method of consecration to Jesus through Mary.

Anselm W. Romb. *Total Consecration to Mary in the Spirit of St. Maximilian Kolbe*. Unlike the Montfort method, which takes thirty-three days, this method, informed by the spirituality of St. Maximillian Kolbe, takes the form of a novena (nine days). Some find it to be an easier method of Marian consecration, for it contains fewer prayers and takes a shorter time to complete.

Appendix Two

Prayers to the Immaculate Heart of Mary

A Solemn Act of Consecration to the Immaculate Heart of Mary

Most Holy Virgin Mary, tender Mother of men, to fulfill the desires of the Sacred Heart of Jesus and the request of the Vicar of Your Son on earth, we consecrate ourselves and our families to your Sorrowful and Immaculate Heart, O Queen of the Most Holy Rosary, and we recommend to You, all the people of our country and all the world. Please accept our consecration, dearest Mother, and use us as You wish to accomplish Your designs in the world.

O Sorrowful and Immaculate Heart of Mary, Queen of the Most Holy Rosary, and Queen of the World, rule over us, together with the Sacred Heart of Jesus Christ, Our King. Save us from the spreading flood of modern paganism; kindle in our hearts and homes the love of purity, the practice of a virtuous life, an ardent zeal for souls, and a desire to pray the Rosary more faithfully.

We come with confidence to You, O Throne of Grace and Mother of Fair Love. Inflame us with the same Divine Fire which has inflamed Your own Sorrowful and Immaculate Heart. Make our hearts and homes Your shrine, and through us, make the Heart of Jesus, together with your rule, triumph in every heart and home.

Amen.[11]

—Venerable Pope Pius XII

Daily Marian Consecration Prayer

My Queen and my Mother, I give myself entirely to you; and to show my devotion to you, I consecrate to you this day my eyes, my ears, my mouth, my heart, my whole being without reserve. Wherefore, good Mother, as I am your own, keep me, guard me, as your property and possession. Amen.[12]

Consecration to the Admirable Heart of Mary

O most holy heart of Mary, ever Immaculate, ever Virgin, holiest, purest, noblest, greatest, inexhaustible fountain of goodness, sweetness, mercy and love; model of every virtue, image of the Adorable Heart of Jesus Christ ever burning with the most ardent charity, who loves God more than all the Seraphim together; Heart of the Mother of the Redeemer, seat of peace, wherein mercy and justice are allied, whence peace between Heaven and earth has begun to be treated, who didst feel our miseries so deeply, who didst suffer so much for our salvation, who still loves us so ardently and who dost merit by all these rights, the respect, love and confidence of all men: deign to accept my poor tribute of love.

Prostrate before thee, I render thee the most profound homage of which I am capable; I thank thee for the feelings of love and mercy with which thou art so deeply moved at the sight of our misery; I offer thee my humble thanks for all the gifts I have received from thy goodness, and I unite with all the pure souls who delight in honoring, praising, and loving thee. They have learned from the Holy Spirit who directs them, that it is through thee they must go to Jesus Christ, and offer to this God-Man their need of adoration.

Therefore, O Most loving Heart, thou shalt henceforth be the object of my veneration, of my love and most tender devotion; thou shalt be the way whereby I shall go to my Savior, as it is through thee that His mercy shall come to me; thou shalt be my refuge in every need, my consolation in every affliction; from thee I shall learn the purity, humility, meekness, and above all, the love of Jesus. I shall ask for these virtues through thy merits and so shall infallibly obtain them. I presume to offer thee my heart sullied with a thousand sins. All unworthy as it is, I trust that thou wilt not despise it. Grant by thy powerful mediation that it may be purified and detached from every creature; penetrate it with sorrow for my sins; fill it with the love of the divine Heart of Jesus, thy Son, that it may be eternally united with thee in Heaven, there to love God forever. Amen.[13]

—St. John Eudes

Prayer to the Immaculate Heart of Mary

O Immaculate Heart of Mary, Heavenly beauty and splendor of the Father, You are the most valued Heavenly treasure.

New Eve, immaculate in soul, spirit and body, Created of the godly seed by the Spirit of God, You are the spiritual Mother of mankind.

Pure Virgin, full of grace then and now, Your whole being was raised Heavenly in full glory, To be elevated above all the hosts within the Kingdom of God.

O Heavenly Mother, Queen of Heaven and earth, I recognize the glory of your highest title, The Immaculate Heart of Mary!

Loving Mother, dispenser of endless blessings, You who continuously intercedes on our behalf, please present my need before your loving Son Jesus.

(In your own words, make your special request here. Do not just mention a word. Speak to the Immaculate Heart of Mary as you would speak to another person, begging your Heavenly Mother to plead to Jesus on your behalf, that you be granted this special request.)

O Immaculate Heart of Mary, I know that you are now presenting my need before Jesus, For you have never turned away those in dire need.

Mother dearest, I await your favorable answer, Submitting myself to the Divine will of the Lord, For all glories are His forever and ever.[14]

Prayer to the Immaculate Heart of Mary

O Immaculate Heart of Mary, full of goodness, show your love towards us. Let the flame of your heart, O Mary, descend on all people. We love you immensely. Impress true love in our hearts so that we have a continuous desire for you. O Mary, gentle and humble of heart, remember us when we are in sin. You know that all men sin. Give us, by means of your Immaculate Heart, spiritual health. Let us always see the goodness of your motherly heart and may we be converted by means of the flame of your heart. Amen.

Immaculate Heart of Mary, full of love for God and mankind, and of compassion for sinners, I consecrate myself to you. I entrust to you the salvation of my soul. May my heart be ever united with yours, so that I may hate sin, love God and my neighbor, and reach eternal life with those whom I love. May I experience the kindness of your motherly heart and the power of your intercession with Jesus during my life and at the hour of my death. Amen.

Prostrate at your sacred feet, O august Queen of Heaven, I venerate you with the most profound respect, and I believe that you are the daughter of the Eternal Father, the Mother of his Divine Son, and the Spouse of the Holy Ghost. Full of grace and virtues and heavenly gifts, you are the purest temple of the most Holy Trinity, you are the treasury and dispenser of divine mercy. Thy Immaculate Heart, full of charity, sweetness and tenderness, has given you the name of Mother of Divine Clemency.

Therefore, in my affliction and agony I present myself with confidence before you, our most loving Mother, and I pray you will help me experience the love which you give us; Grant me (specify the favor) if it be the will of God and for the good of my soul. Amen.

O Immaculate Heart of Mary, refuge of sinners, I beg of you by the infinite merits of the Sacred Heart of Jesus, and by the graces God has granted to you since your Immaculate Conception, the grace of never going astray again. Mother, keep me, a sinner, constantly bathed in the light of your Immaculate Heart. Amen.[15]

Prayer of St. Teresa of Calcutta

Mary, my dearest Mother, give me your heart, so beautiful, so pure, so immaculate, so full of love and humility, that I may receive Jesus as you did and go in haste to give Him to others.[16]

Prayer to Our Lady of Beauraing

Our Lady of Beauraing, Immaculate Virgin, ever victorious in all thy battles for the kingdom of God, we beseech thee, convert sinners, as thou hast promised.

Exercise in their behalf the power of thy Immaculate Heart! Bring back to the love of God all souls who, deprived of sanctifying grace, stand in danger of eternal perdition.

O Heavenly Mother, cast thine eyes of mercy on thy poor children, and be our Help in all tribulations! Be thou the Health of the sick and Comforter of the Afflicted.

Queen of Heaven, crowned with eternal glory, our love and our gratitude proclaim thee also Queen of our hearts and Sovereign of the world. We shall work for the extension of thy kingdom in ourselves, by sacrifice and imitation of thy virtues; and around us by frequent prayers and good works.

May thou reign over the whole world and spread everywhere the kingdom of thy Son, Our Lord Jesus Christ. Amen.

Our Father ... Hail Mary ... Glory be to the Father.
Our Lady of Beauraing, convert sinners.
Queen of the Golden Heart, help the sick.[17]

Morning Offering

O Jesus, through the Immaculate Heart of Mary, I offer thee all my prayers, works, and sufferings of this day for all the intentions of thy Sacred Heart, in union with the Holy Sacrifice of the Mass throughout the world, in reparation for my sins, for the intentions of all our associates, and in particular for the intention of the Holy Father.

Notes

1. "Nican Mopohua: Original Account of Guadalupe," in *A Handbook on Guadalupe* (New Bedford, MA: Academy of the Immaculata, 1997), 194.

2. *Fatima in Lucia's Own Words: Sister Lucia's Memoirs*, 19th ed., ed. Louis Kondor, XVD (Fatima, Portugal: Postulation Center, 2014), Second Memoir, 78.

3. Sister Dominica, *Chapel of Our Lady of Good Help: A History* (1955): 8–9/(2014): 20–21.

4. Don Sharkey and Joseph Debergh, *Our Lady of Beauraing* (Garden City: NYL Hanover House, 1958), 223.

5. Don Sharkey, *The Woman Shall Conquer* (Libertyville, IL: Franciscan Marytown Press, 1986), 134.

6. Sharkey and Debergh, *Our Lady of Beauraing,* 223.

7. *Fatima in Lucia's Own Words: Sister Lucia's Memoirs*, Fourth Memoir, 176.

8. *Fatima in Lucia's Own Words: Sister Lucia's Memoirs*, Fourth Memoir, 178.

9. List adapted from Mark Miravalle, "Marian Private Revelations: Nature, Evaluation, Message," in *Mariology: A Guide for Priests, Deacons, Seminarians, and Consecrated Persons*, ed. Mark Miraville (Goleta, CA: Seat of Wisdom Books, 2007), 879.

10. *Fatima in Lucia's Own Words: Sister Lucia's Memoirs*, Fourth Memoir, 179.

11. "A Solemn Act of Consecration to the Immaculate Heart of Mary," EWTN, https://www.ewtn.com/Devotionals/heart/Im_consecr.htm.

12. "Consecration to Mary," Catholic Online, http://www.catholic.org/prayers/prayer.php?p=536.

13. St. John Eudes, *The Admirable Heart of Mary*, trans. Charles di Targiani and Ruth Hauser (Fitzwilliam, NH: Loreto Publications, 2006), 378.

14. "Prayer to the Immaculate Heart of Mary," Catholic Online, http://www.catholic.org/prayers/prayer.php?p=2222.

15. "Hail Holy Queen," Prayers to Mary, http://www.marypages.com/PrayerstoMary.htm.

16. From her speech to youth in Naples, May 11, 1996.

17. Sharkey and Debergh, *Our Lady of Beauraing*, 225.

Rev. Edward Looney is a Marian theologian and Catholic author and speaker who serves as a priest in the Diocese of Green Bay.

Looney earned his bachelor's degree in philosophy in 2011 from Conception Seminary College. He also received a bachelor's degree in sacred theology and a master's degree in divinity from the University of St. Mary of the Lake/Mundelein Seminary.

In 2007, Looney received the Sharon Schumer Pro-Life Award. He is a member of the Thomas Merton Society and the Mariological Society of America, where he was elected to be a councilor in 2015. He is the author of seven books. He has contributed to numerous publications, including *Catholic Digest*, *Catholic Exchange*, *Ignitum Today*, *Catholic Lane*, and *Homiletic* and *Pastoral Review*. He also has appeared on EWTN TV and Radio, Relevant Radio, the Catholic Channel on SiriusXM Radio, Spirit Radio, Mater Dei Radio, and Radio Maria.

AVE

AVE MARIA PRESS

Founded in 1865, Ave Maria Press,
a ministry of the Congregation of
Holy Cross, is a Catholic publishing
company that serves the spiritual and
formative needs of the Church and its
schools, institutions, and ministers;
Christian individuals and families; and
others seeking spiritual nourishment.

For a complete listing of titles from

Ave Maria Press

Sorin Books

Forest of Peace

Christian Classics

visit www.avemariapress.com

AVE MARIA PRESS
Notre Dame, IN
A Ministry of the United States Province of Holy Cross